50 States

G...
to Comple... ...rriculum

Grades 3-5

by
Shirley Pearson

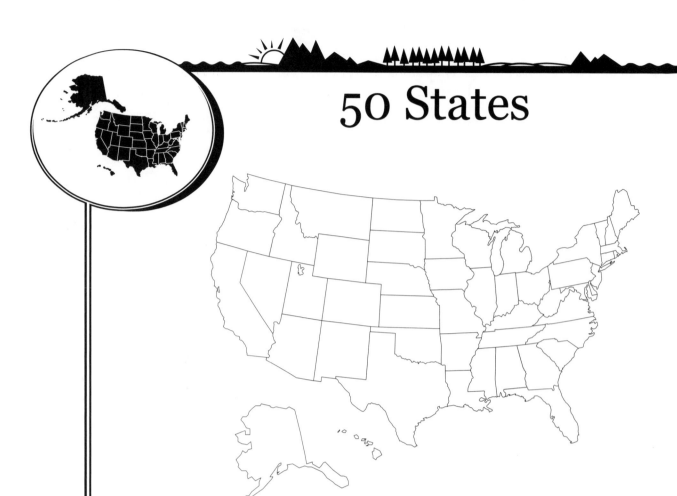

50 States

Editors:	Kelly Gunzenhauser
	Kim Fields
Layout Design:	Mark Conrad
Illustrations:	Betsy Peninger
Cover Design:	Dez Beckwith
Cover Photos:	Photo www.comstock.com
	Mountain High Maps®
	© 1993 Digital Wisdom, Inc.

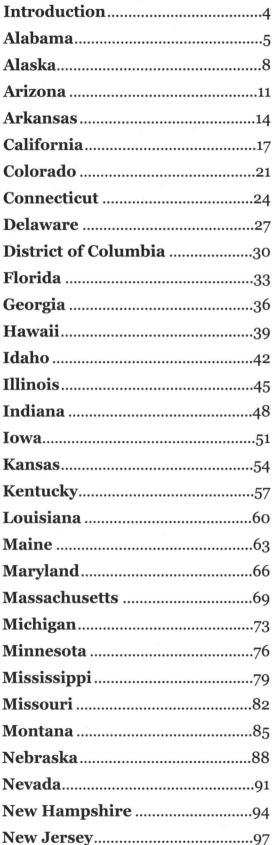

TABLE OF CONTENTS

INTRODUCTION

Did you know that no one believed early descriptions of what is now Yellowstone National Park? Or that the Outer Banks of North Carolina were the hideout of a ferocious pirate called Blackbeard? Have you ever heard that Texas was an independent country at one time? These and other interesting facts found in *50 States* will take students on a journey to far-away and exotic cities, exciting time periods from the past, and geographical wonders—all right here in the United States.

Learning about individual states has always been an integral part of elementary and middle school curriculums. This exciting resource reaches well beyond fact memorization. It combines high-interest reading passages with reading comprehension questions designed to help students learn more about each state and the District of Columbia. The reading passages focus on government, history, population, geography, industry, notable people, and even foreign languages. Students will learn state nicknames and their origins, relative sizes and bordering states, geographical features, and many unusual facts. Each Reading Comprehension page includes space for students to record state symbols (listed on page 164). Each Comprehension Questions page also includes a "What do you think?" question, which encourages students to think critically.

Additionally, each state chapter includes a fun activity page. There are crosswords, word searches, scrambled words, graphs, math activities, and more—all designed to teach unusual state facts. Many of these pages require the use of atlases, encyclopedias, almanacs, and other resources. Students will enjoy the variety of activities and the research they will need to do in order to find answers.

So grab an atlas and prepare to take a trip around the *50 States*. Meet the people, visit the places, and participate in the customs that make each state unique. And, teach students what is special about their home state as well. They will be sure to appreciate the great state and country they call home.

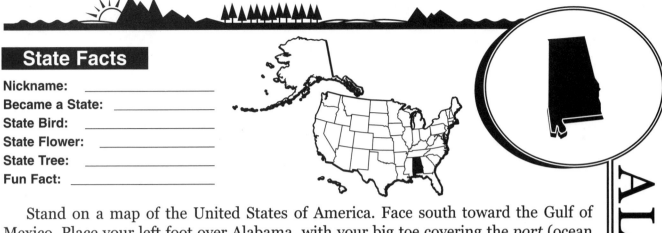

State Facts

Nickname: _____

Became a State: _____

State Bird: _____

State Flower: _____

State Tree: _____

Fun Fact: _____

Stand on a map of the United States of America. Face south toward the Gulf of Mexico. Place your left foot over Alabama, with your big toe covering the *port* (ocean harbor) city of Mobile. Can you feel the "Heart of Dixie" beating beneath your toes?

Before becoming America's 22nd state in 1819, Alabama was a colony of France, Britain, and Spain. Although Alabama didn't play a major role in the American Revolution, it was a key player in the Civil War of the 1860s. The capital of the break-away Confederate States was located in Montgomery. That city remains the state's capital today.

Most of southern Alabama lies close to sea level. This low plain is covered in grass-land suitable for cotton, peanut, and soybean crops. The southwestern piece of land (under your big toe) includes 50 miles of coastline in the swampy *delta* (river mouth) around Mobile Bay. Traveling northward (toward your heel) brings you into hilly terrain. In the northwest, pine forests reach to the Tennessee border. The Appalachian Mountains are the oldest mountain system in North America. This 1,500 mile-long mountain chain runs northeast from Birmingham, Alabama, into eastern Canada. The ridges and valleys of these hills contain coal, limestone, and iron ore—important ingredients in Birmingham's steel industry. Large natural lakes in Alabama are few, but rivers are plenty, crisscrossing the state in all directions.

Alabama is not just a state of steel and cotton. In 1915, farmers started to plant peanuts and other crops after the boll weevil beetle nearly wiped out the cotton crop. The first men on the moon used rockets built by scientists from Huntsville, Alabama (also known as "Rocket City"). The twentieth-century Civil Rights movement started in Alabama.

As you're standing on Alabama, Tennessee is behind you to the north; Florida is in front of you to the south; Georgia is on your left to the east; and Mississippi is on your right to the west. Alabama is truly the "Heart of Dixie."

ALABAMA

A...L...A...B...A...M...A

Learn more about the state of Alabama. Use an atlas or encyclopedia to help you fill in the blanks in the sentences below. Each of the missing words starts with the corresponding letter in the name Alabama.

A The historic battle in 1814 between the troops of General A __ __ __ __ __ Jackson ("Old Hickory") and the Creek Indians can be revisited at Horseshoe Bend National Military Park.

L Civil War hero General Robert E. L __ __'s birthday is celebrated in Alabama on the third Monday in January.

A Cheaha Mountain in Talladega National Forest is the highest point in Alabama. This mountain lies just south of the city of A __ __ __ __ __ __ __.

B The words from Martin Luther King Jr.'s "Letter from a B __ __ __ __ __ __ __ __ __ Jail," written in 1963, still have truth today: "Injustice anywhere is a threat to justice everywhere."

A The "A __ __ __ __ __ __ __ __ __ South" refers to the southern states prior to the time of the American Civil War.

M The Civil Rights movement of the mid-twentieth century can be traced back to M __ __ __ __ __ __ __ __ __, Alabama, in 1955, when Rosa Parks' refusal to give up her bus seat set off an unstoppable chain of events.

A Although the Camellia is Alabama's state flower, it is another flowering shrub called an a __ __ __ __ __ that is the namesake of a picturesque trail that runs through the city of Mobile.

Comprehension Questions

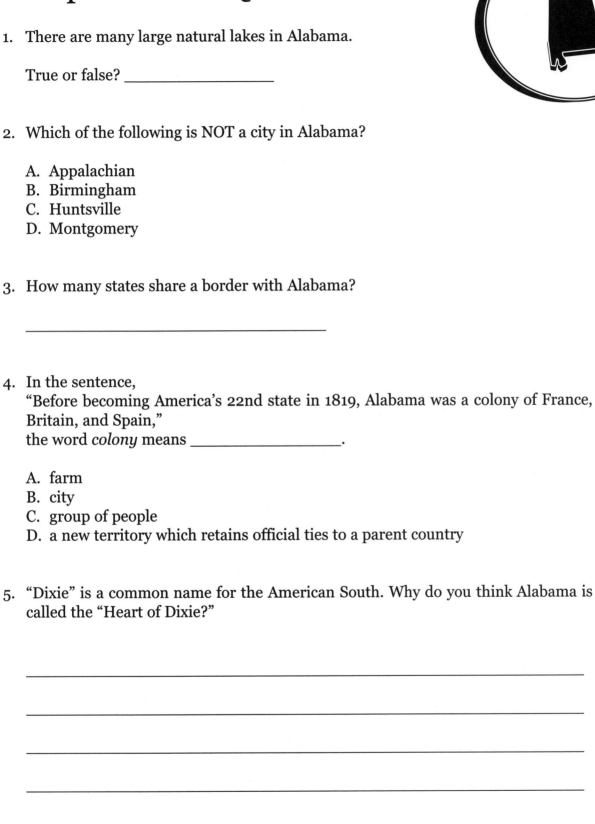

1. There are many large natural lakes in Alabama.

    True or false? _____

2. Which of the following is NOT a city in Alabama?

    A. Appalachian
    B. Birmingham
    C. Huntsville
    D. Montgomery

3. How many states share a border with Alabama?

    _____

4. In the sentence,
    "Before becoming America's 22nd state in 1819, Alabama was a colony of France,
    Britain, and Spain,"
    the word *colony* means _____.

    A. farm
    B. city
    C. group of people
    D. a new territory which retains official ties to a parent country

5. "Dixie" is a common name for the American South. Why do you think Alabama is
    called the "Heart of Dixie?"

    _____

    _____

    _____

    _____

    _____

ALABAMA

ALASKA

State Facts

Nickname: _____

Became a State: _____

State Bird: _____

State Flower: _____

State Tree: _____

Fun Fact: _____

You don't have a pilot's license? How can you see Alaska without one? Do you have a car? You could take the Alaska Highway and drive west through Canada to the central town of Fairbanks. What about a train? You could head for the big city of Anchorage. Don't forget the ferry! You could sail up from Seattle, Washington, to Juneau, Alaska's capital. But if you want to see all of Alaska, you really need a plane, and lots of fuel.

Alaska is one-sixth the size of the entire United States. It has more lakes, glaciers, and volcanoes than any other state. Alaska's Mount McKinley is North America's tallest mountain. You can't drive to small towns in the *interior* (land far from borders or oceans) because mountains block the way. However, you can fly. Nearly every community has a landing strip. That's all a bush pilot needs.

Alaska is America's "Land of the Midnight Sun." The northern third of Alaska lies within the Arctic Circle. For several weeks in the summer, the sun never sets, but winters on the treeless *tundra* (arctic plains) are dark. Alaska's interior is extremely cold in winter. The coastal areas are milder but receive more rain and snow.

Alaska's mainland is only 50 miles from Russia. Alaska was already populated when Russian explorers first visited in 1741. Native Alaskans lived near the Bering Sea and Arctic Ocean. Tlingit and Haida tribes fished along the southeastern coast. Athabascan Indians roamed the mountains. Aleuts ruled the Aleutian Islands. After the fur trade died out, Russia lost interest. In 1867, the land was purchased from Russia by the United States, thanks to negotiations by William H. Seward, Secretary of State to President Abraham Lincoln. Americans weren't interested in Alaska, either—until the 1880 gold rush. Gold mines, forests for logging, and waters full of fish persuaded the American government to make Alaska an official territory. In 1959, Alaska became the 49th state.

In Alaska, gold isn't as important as it once was. *Petroleum* (oil) is the new king, followed by tourism. As you would see from a plane, Alaska is America's last great wilderness. Flying is easy; conserving Alaska's wilderness is much harder.

Alaska's Many Waters

Over 70% of the Earth is covered in salt water. We divide this water into four main oceans: the Atlantic, Pacific, Indian, and Arctic. Two of these oceans meet at Alaska.

Below the map, there are words that describe different bodies of water. Read each definition and the Alaskan examples. Then, use an atlas or encyclopedia to help you fill in the letter of each missing body of water on the map of Alaska below.

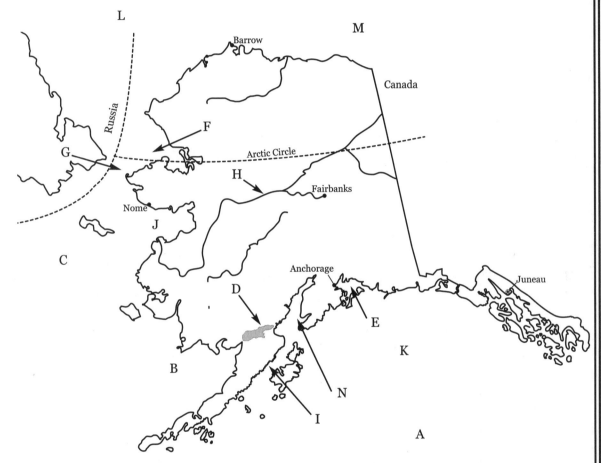

Ocean: Any of seven large bodies of salt water which circle the Earth
(___ Arctic Ocean, ___ Pacific Ocean)

Sea: Part of an ocean that is partially enclosed by land (___ Beaufort Sea, ___ Bering Sea)

Gulf: Large arm of the ocean that extends into land (___ Gulf of Alaska)

Bay: Same as a gulf, but smaller (___ Bristol Bay)

Inlet: Same as a bay, but smaller and narrower (___ Cook Inlet)

Sound: Long, broad inlet which usually runs parallel to the coastline; also, the strip of water between the mainland and an island or group of islands
(___ Kotzebue Sound, ___ Norton Sound, ___ Prince William Sound)

Strait: Narrow strip of water that joins two larger bodies of water
(___ Bering Strait, ___ Shelikof Strait)

Lake: An inland body of fresh- or saltwater (___ Iliamna Lake)

River: Water which moves across the land from lakes to oceans (___ Yukon River)

Comprehension Questions

1. Fairbanks is the capital of Alaska.

   True or false? _____

2. What portion of Alaska lies within the Arctic Circle?

   A. All
   B. None
   C. One-half
   D. One-third

3. How many years after the first Russian explorers visited Alaska did Alaska become a U.S. state?

   _____

4. In the sentence,
   "Gold mines, forests for logging, and waters full of fish persuaded the American government to make Alaska an official territory,"
   the word *persuaded* means _____.

   A. convinced
   B. found
   C. showed
   D. wanted

5. Alaska is called the "Land of the Midnight Sun." Can you think of another similar nickname ("Land of the _____") that might describe Alaska's winters? Explain why you chose your nickname.

   _____

   _____

   _____

   _____

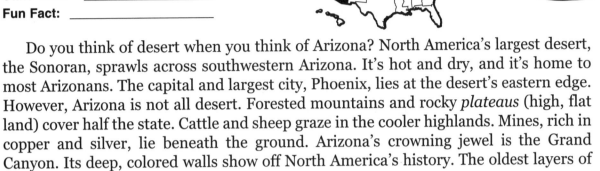

State Facts

Nickname: _____

Became a State: _____

State Bird: _____

State Flower: _____

State Tree: _____

Fun Fact: _____

ARIZONA

Do you think of desert when you think of Arizona? North America's largest desert, the Sonoran, sprawls across southwestern Arizona. It's hot and dry, and it's home to most Arizonans. The capital and largest city, Phoenix, lies at the desert's eastern edge. However, Arizona is not all desert. Forested mountains and rocky *plateaus* (high, flat land) cover half the state. Cattle and sheep graze in the cooler highlands. Mines, rich in copper and silver, lie beneath the ground. Arizona's crowning jewel is the Grand Canyon. Its deep, colored walls show off North America's history. The oldest layers of rock in the canyon are two billion years old.

Native Americans have lived in Arizona for hundreds of years. The Hohokam farmed the Salt River Valley. The Anasazi lived in northern canyon cliffs. The Mogollon hunted in the east. The Navajo and Apache Indians joined these earlier groups. Many of these tribes live on Arizona's reservations today.

Arizona was first conquered by Spain. When Mexico declared independence from Spain in 1821, Mexico claimed Arizona. After America's victory in the Mexican War, Arizona became part of the United States. The Navajo and Apache Indians resisted white settlement until 1886, when Apache chief Geronimo surrendered. In 1912, Arizona became the 48th state. Today, one-fourth of Arizona is Indian Reservation. The Navajo Reserve is the largest in the country.

Arizona's climate is good . . . and bad. Good, because people visit and move to Arizona for the warm weather and dry air. But the *arid* (dry) climate also makes water scarce. Many rivers run dry. Arizonans have always struggled with water. The Hohokam dug ditches to direct water to their crops. This first irrigation system allowed them to move water to the desert and plant crops in the desert soil. Farmers in desert valleys still successfully grow cotton and citrus fruits. The Hoover and Roosevelt Dams have created huge lakes. These lakes, plus snow run-off from mountains and the Colorado River, provide Arizona with much-needed water for people and crops.

ARIZONA

Life in the Desert

Arizona is full of life. Many plants and animals have adapted to the desert environment. One of these animals is the *collared peccary* (a type of wild pig).

Some plants and animals native to Arizona are listed in the word bank below. Find and circle each of these words in the Wild Pig Puzzle. (Hint: Names with more than one word will be found together in the puzzle.)

In the top eight horizontal rows, circle the first unused letter. These letters, in order, will spell another name for the peccary:

____ __ ____ _____ ____ _____ ____ ____

Word Bank

Animals
bald eagle
bass
collared peccary
coyote
desert tortoise
rattlesnake
scorpion

Plants
cholla cactus
creosote bush
prickly pear
saguaro blossom
succulents
yucca plant

Crops
alfalfa
chiles
cotton
dates
grapefruit
grapes

Livestock
cattle
sheep

Wild Pig Puzzle

```
J  R  P  R  I  C  K  L  Y  P  E  A  R  J  W  Y  E
A  U  K  Y  S  C  O  T  T  O  N  J  X  B  R  L  O
C  C  V  A  O  D  A  T  E  S  Y  M  X  A  G  C  C
S  R  A  E  I  S  T  L  H  H  J  D  C  A  Y  H  D
U  L  E  T  R  E  A  F  V  E  K  C  E  G  U  O  E
C  I  J  O  T  Q  G  T  B  E  E  D  J  R  C  L  S
C  N  Y  G  S  L  A  T  J  P  L  R  W  A  C  L  E
U  A  W  J  A  O  E  K  D  A  F  N  X  P  A  A  R
L  R  Z  Z  R  Q  T  E  B  D  Q  V  Z  E  P  C  T
E  A  A  I  W  E  R  E  S  R  D  V  A  F  L  A  T
N  T  R  S  T  A  A  J  B  C  S  A  C  R  A  C  O
T  A  S  O  L  F  X  O  P  U  O  A  P  U  N  T  R
S  A  Y  L  L  G  R  A  P  E  S  R  H  I  T  U  T
B  O  O  A  D  W  F  S  H  U  I  H  P  T  Z  S  O
C  C  F  B  V  C  H  I  L  E  S  A  L  I  G  D  I
K  L  R  A  T  T  L  E  S  N  A  K  E  S  O  Q  S
A  S  A  G  U  A  R  O  B  L  O  S  S  O  M  N  E
```

Comprehension Questions

1. The Sonoran Desert is located in southwestern Arizona.

   True or false? _____

2. When did Arizona become a state?

   A. 1821
   B. 1886
   C. 1912
   D. 1948

3. What crops are grown in Arizona?

   _____   _____

4. In the sentence,
   "The Navajo and Apache Indians resisted white settlement,"
   the word *resisted* means _____.

   A. disliked
   B. fought against
   C. looked for
   D. wanted

5. The Grand Canyon is one of the seven natural wonders of the world. In some places, the canyon is one mile deep. The canyon is very wide, which makes its walls visible. The Colorado River runs through the canyon. Over millions of years, the rushing water has *eroded* (cut through) the rock surrounding it. What can the walls of the canyon tell us about the past?

   _____

   _____

   _____

ARKANSAS

State Facts

Nickname: _____
Became a State: _____
State Bird: _____
State Flower: _____
State Tree: _____
Fun Fact: _____

The name "Arkansas" was written as *Arkansa*, *Arkansaw*, and *Arkansea*. In 1836, when Arkansas became the 25th state, residents agreed upon the spelling *Arkansas*. However, it was another 45 years before they decided how to pronounce it! The river that cuts across the entire state is also called the Arkansas. Arkansas is named for the Quapaw Indians, who lived along the Arkansas River. (The word *Quapaw* means "downstream people.") The Quapaw, Caddo, and Osage tribes lived there when the Spanish arrived in 1541. Although white settlement forced the Quapaw westward, the name remained.

In the northwest, the Arkansas River Valley separates the Ozark *Plateau* (highland) from the forested Ouachita (**Wa**-shi-ta) Mountains. Fruit orchards and *poultry* (chicken) farms are found throughout the Ozarks. Hot springs bubble up from the ground, as do oil and natural gas. The cliffs and caves of Arkansas' mountains are very beautiful. Little Rock, the capital, lies in the middle of the state, between the high mountains and the low plains.

All the rivers in Arkansas flow downstream, forever chasing the great Mississippi. The Arkansas River which flows across the state is a *tributary* (a smaller river flowing into a larger river) of the Mississippi River. The Mississippi forms Arkansas' eastern border. The Arkansas River is not the only large tributary in the state. The White River runs down from the Ozark Plateau. It joins with the Arkansas just before flowing into the Mississippi. The Ouachita River and Red River head south through Louisiana before reaching the Mississippi. This web of rivers feeds Arkansas' rich soil. Warm temperatures, plenty of rain, and a long growing season also help. Pick a crop, any crop. If it grows anywhere in the country, chances are it grows in Arkansas.

These same helpful rivers can also destroy. Flooding is a serious problem. For hundreds of years, farmers have worked to turn the river swampland into farmland. They build ditches and *levees* (high blockades along river banks) to control the rising waters. Often, the river wins. During the great flood of 1927, over one-tenth of Arkansas was under water.

What Comes Next in Arkansas?

A time line and a list of important events in Arkansas' history are shown below. Each event is labeled with a letter. Use an encyclopedia or another resource to research these events. List the events in *chronological order* (in order of occurrence) on the timeline by filling in each box with the appropriate event letter. When you are finished, the letters in the boxes will spell the name of the Arkansas state bird.

I   Arkansas became a state.

D   Little Rock Central High School made the decision to accept African-American students, in the face of protests from the governor and many people in the community.

N   Arkansas changed its constitution, allowing black people the right to vote.

K   Little Rock became the territorial capital of Arkansas.

M   Spanish explorer, Hernando de Soto, visited Arkansas.

C   The Arkansas area was included in the Louisiana Purchase, becoming part of the United States.

I   The "Great Flood" of this year affected seven states. Over 100 people in Arkansas lost their lives, and 13% of the state was covered with water.

O   The first permanent European settlement (Arkansas Post) in Arkansas was established.

G   Douglas MacArthur, future Five-Star U.S. Army General and supreme commander of the Allied forces in World War II, was born in Little Rock.

R   The future 42nd president of the United States, Bill Clinton, was born in Hope, Arkansas.

B   Sam Walton, who would go on to found Wal-Mart® stores, was born in Newport.

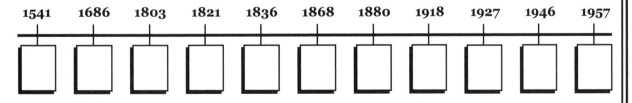

1541	1686	1803	1821	1836	1868	1880	1918	1927	1946	1957

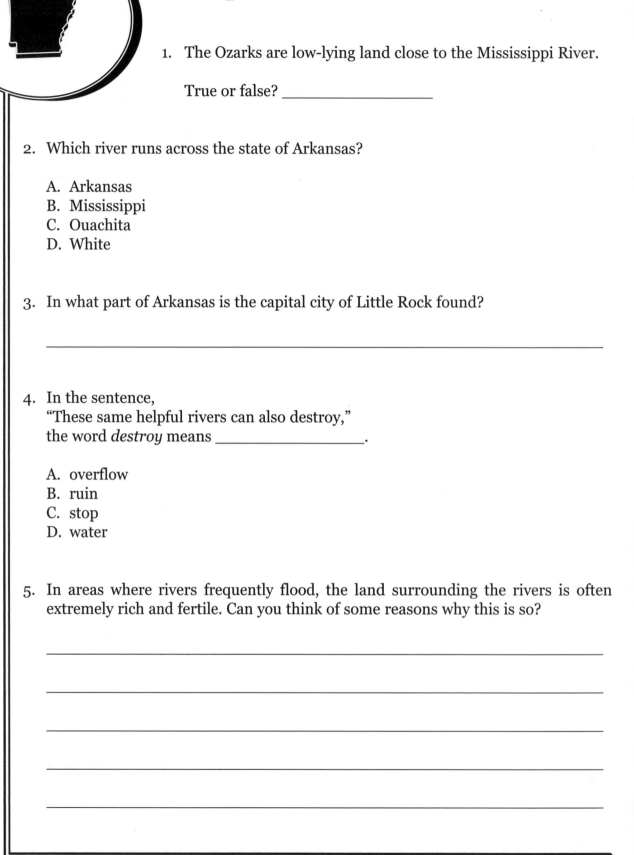

Comprehension Questions

ARKANSAS

1. The Ozarks are low-lying land close to the Mississippi River.

    True or false? _____

2. Which river runs across the state of Arkansas?

    A. Arkansas
    B. Mississippi
    C. Ouachita
    D. White

3. In what part of Arkansas is the capital city of Little Rock found?

    _____

4. In the sentence,
    "These same helpful rivers can also destroy,"
    the word *destroy* means _____.

    A. overflow
    B. ruin
    C. stop
    D. water

5. In areas where rivers frequently flood, the land surrounding the rivers is often extremely rich and fertile. Can you think of some reasons why this is so?

    _____

    _____

    _____

    _____

    _____

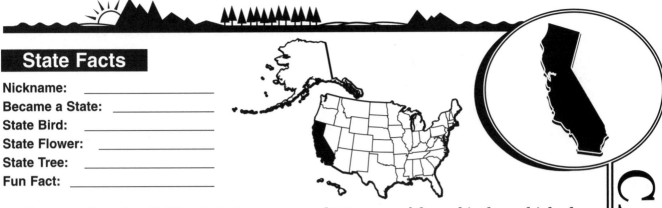

State Facts

Nickname: _____

Became a State: _____

State Bird: _____

State Flower: _____

State Tree: _____

Fun Fact: _____

Can you describe California in just one word? Try one of these: big, busy, high, dry, wet, sunny, bumpy. Or, would you describe the state using a culture, such as Native American, Mexican, or Spanish? The state of California cannot be summed up in just one word, because it's simply all of the above!

Forty-seven states are smaller than California—only Texas and Alaska are bigger. More people live in California than in any other state. Almost everybody lives in an urban area, and there are many large cities to choose from: Los Angeles, San Francisco, San Diego, and Oakland, to name a few.

California has mountains with record-tall redwoods, snowy ski slopes, and even active volcanoes! The Sierra Nevada is the highest mountain range of them all. This stony mountain range runs along California's eastern border. It is crowned by Mount Whitney, the country's second-highest peak.

California has both a wet and dry climate because the state covers so much area. Some early travelers had to cross the Mojave Desert in southeastern California. If they were lucky enough to survive the crossing, they had Death Valley (which is very hot and dry) to look forward to! On the other hand, northern California has rushing rivers and plenty of rain. California's challenge is to move this extra water to the dry south.

This state is also a surfer's paradise. Over 800 miles of Pacific coastline are lined with sandy beaches and scenic cliffs. The weather is warm; the winters are mild. Although California is a wonderful place to be, living in California can be very shaky at times! As scary as it seems, earthquakes are common occurrences.

The first explorers encountered over 100 different Native American tribes in California. The Spanish established the earliest non-Native American settlements along the coast. Spain lost control of California when Mexico became independent in 1822. However, Mexican rule was short-lived. In 1850, at the heart of the Gold Rush, California became the 31st state. At that time, "Miner 49ers" were stampeding to California, hoping to strike it rich. That stampede continues even today, because California has the largest percentage of citizens that were born elsewhere.

California Code

Use an atlas, encyclopedia, or another resource to help you complete the crossword puzzle.

CALIFORNIA

Across

2. In the 1700s, missionaries from this country established missions along California's coast.
4. _ _ _ Angeles is the largest city in California.
6. The San Gabriel and San Bernadino Mountains run east-west, and are part of this mountain range.
10. This island in San Francisco Bay was once a famous prison.
11. These letters are California's postal code.
12. The name of the mountain ranges closest to Redwood National Forest.
15. This central California valley is famous for its vineyards.
16. The country's largest desert.
17. The Spanish word for the California mainland above Baja California.
19. This is the name of a central California valley and the surrounding National Park, which are both found in the Sierra Nevada.
22. What the 49ers were looking for.
24. San Francisco Bay separates San Francisco from this large city.
25. _ _ _ _ Tahoe, on the California-Nevada border, is one of the deepest in the country.
26. You can visit Mickey Mouse® at Walt _ _ _ _ _ _'s theme park in Anaheim.

Down

1. Many actors live in the Beverly _ _ _ _ _ neighborhood of Los Angeles.
3. In 1906, the city of San _ _ _ _ _ _ _ _ _ was struck by a devastating earthquake. The resulting fire destroyed much of the city.
5. California's northern neighbor.
6. Abbreviation for Los Angeles.
7. _ _ _ Diego
8. The Spanish name of this city means "Saint Joseph."
9. Army officer John _ _ _ _ _ _ _ was an explorer. In 1843, he and scout Kit Carson crossed the Sierra Nevada.
12. "El _ _ _ _ _ _ Real" (the royal road) was an 18th-century path that connected Spanish missions along the California coast.
13. Death _ _ _ _ _ _, the lowest place on the continent, lies 282 feet below sea level.
14. Some of the world's largest Sequoia trees are found in King's _ _ _ _ _ _ National Park.
18. The San _ _ _ _ _ _ _ Fault causes many earthquakes.
20. The _ _ _ _ _ _ Sea is a large, inland sea in the Colorado Desert of southern California. It was formed in 1905 by the flooding of the Colorado River.
21. The Farallon _ _ _ _ _ _ _ are off the coast of San Francisco.
22. The immense Sierra Redwood tree is also called the _ _ _ _ _ Sequoia.
23. Spanish conqueror Hernando _ _ _ _ _ _ was the first explorer to use the word "California."

California Code

CALIFORNIA

What is the largest flying bird in North America? Use the first letters of your clue answers to find out.

___ ___ ___ ___ ___ ___ R N ___ ___   ___ ___ N ___ ___ R
12A 17A 6D 21D 3D 24A   21D 18D   14D 24A   26A 24A

Due to hunting and habitat destruction, by the 1980s, less than 25 of these graceful vultures remained in the wild. In an attempt to save the species, biologists captured these birds and bred them in captivity. The young birds are now being returned successfully to the wilderness of California and surrounding areas.

Comprehension Questions

1. California is the third largest state in the country.

   True or false? _____

2. What is the name of a large Californian desert?

   A. California
   B. Mojave
   C. Sacramento
   D. Sierra

3. What is the name of a major mountain range in California?

   _____

4. In the sentence,
   "The first explorers encountered over 100 different Native American tribes in California,"
   the word *encountered* means _____.

   A. lived with
   B. met
   C. ran away from
   D. taught

5. California is nicknamed the "Golden State." The word *Gold* can represent something that is very important to us. Give three reasons why you think this nickname is appropriate for California.

   _____

   _____

   _____

   _____

   _____

   _____

CALIFORNIA

State Facts

Nickname: _____
Became a State: _____
State Bird: _____
State Flower: _____
State Tree: _____
Fun Fact: _____

If you're scared of heights, watch out for Colorado! The Rockies run right through the state. Colorado's Mount Elbert is the tallest mountain in the entire Rocky Mountain Range. It's not just Colorado's mountains that are high. Colorado's "lowlands" are high, too. The lowest place in the state is along the Arkansas River—more than 3,000 feet above sea level. That's higher than the tallest mountains in 19 other states!

The Rockies don't cover all of Colorado. The eastern third of the state is part of the Great Plains. Although still high above sea level, it is flat, and also very dry. Farmers grow wheat and corn and raise beef cattle. Much of eastern Colorado's water comes from the mountains through specially built tunnels. Most Coloradans live in cities (including Denver, the capital) at the eastern edge of the Rockies.

The western part of the state, the Colorado Plateau, is higher than the plains but not as high as the mountains. This plateau is filled with canyons, valleys, and *mesas* (flat-topped hills). Ranchers herd cattle and sheep in the mountain valleys. Many important rivers start in Colorado's mountains. Water from the Colorado River, the Arkansas River, and the Rio Grande (Big River) is so precious that there are laws to stop the state of Colorado from taking more than its share.

Spanish explorers first came to Colorado in search of gold. The Spaniards found Arapaho and Cheyenne tribes on the plains. They found Ute tribes high in the mountains. But they didn't find gold. After the 1803 Louisiana Purchase, Americans started to explore Colorado. Settlement did not start until the discovery of gold and silver in the mid-19th century. The Arapaho and Cheyenne were forced onto reservations in other states. Only the Ute remain in Colorado.

Don't let your fear of heights stop you from visiting Colorado. You'll love the scenery, the cool climate, the mountain climbing, and the healthy air. And, you will especially love the skiing. If you listen hard, you'll hear the deep powdery snow of Colorado's winter resorts say, "Time to ski!"

C...O...L...O...R...A...D...O

Learn more about the state of Colorado. Use a dictionary, encyclopedia, or atlas to help you unscramble the mixed-up words in the sentences below. Each of the missing words starts with the corresponding letter in the name Colorado.

C The only place in the country where four states meet is in the southwestern corner of Colorado, where Colorado meets Utah, Arizona, and New Mexico. This meeting place is marked with the Four C __ __ __ __ __ __ Monument.

O The town of O __ __ __ __ in southwestern Colorado is named for a well-loved chief of the Native American Ute tribe. The tribal chief's name meant "The Arrow."

L In 1893, poet Katharine L __ __ Bates of Massachusetts visited Pike's Peak in Colorado. Pike's Peak is one of the easiest mountains to climb in the Rockies, even though it is over 14,000 feet above sea level, and cars can now drive to the top. The view from the summit of this mountain inspired Katharine to write the words to "America the Beautiful."

O Large quantities of o __ __ shale are found in northwestern Colorado. When you heat this rock, you get petroleum and natural gas. It takes a lot of this shale to generate a little bit of fuel, and the heating process is very expensive.

R Cañon City, in south central Colorado, lies along the Arkansas River in an area surrounded by canyons. The bridge over the R __ __ __ __ Gorge canyon, just west of the city, is one of the world's highest suspension bridges. It hangs over 1,000 feet above the Arkansas River.

A A __ __ __ __ is a popular ski town in Colorado's Sawatch Mountains (part of the Rocky Mountain Range). One hundred years ago, this town was rich in silver. In 1893, lucky miners found a silver nugget that weighed almost 2,000 pounds—that's as heavy as a buffalo!

D The city of D __ __ __ __ __, also known as the "Mile High City," was built on the eastern edge of the Rocky Mountains, exactly one mile (5,280 feet) above sea level. Before Colorado became an independent state, this city was in Kansas Territory.

O Leadville, a town in central Colorado, was originally named O __ __ (meaning gold, in Latin) City for the gold that was found in the area in 1860. The gold soon ran out. But in the 1870s, miners discovered silver in the heavy black sand around the city. This black sand was really carbonate of lead, so the town's name was changed to Leadville.

Comprehension Questions

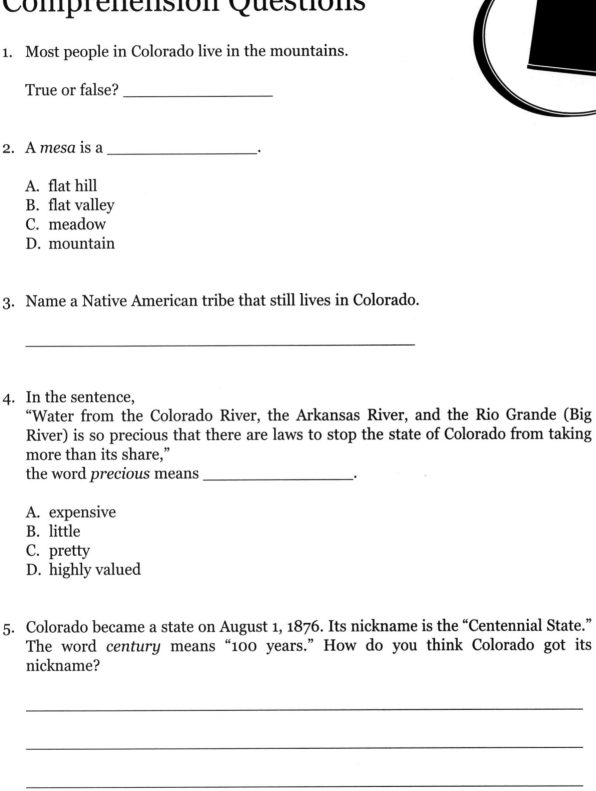

COLORADO

1. Most people in Colorado live in the mountains.

   True or false? _____

2. A *mesa* is a _____.

   A. flat hill
   B. flat valley
   C. meadow
   D. mountain

3. Name a Native American tribe that still lives in Colorado.

   _____

4. In the sentence,
   "Water from the Colorado River, the Arkansas River, and the Rio Grande (Big River) is so precious that there are laws to stop the state of Colorado from taking more than its share,"
   the word *precious* means _____.

   A. expensive
   B. little
   C. pretty
   D. highly valued

5. Colorado became a state on August 1, 1876. Its nickname is the "Centennial State." The word *century* means "100 years." How do you think Colorado got its nickname?

   _____

   _____

   _____

   _____

State Facts

Nickname: _____

Became a State: _____

State Bird: _____

State Flower: _____

State Tree: _____

Fun Fact: _____

Did you know that Connecticut once stretched from the Atlantic to the Pacific? In 1662, England granted a *charter* (document of rights) to the Connecticut Colony. This charter included a strip of land running across the entire continent! At that time, no one knew how big North America really was. Connecticut became the fifth state in 1788. It gave this extra land to the government. If it hadn't, Connecticut would be the third largest state in the nation instead of the third smallest!

The Connecticut River *bisects* (divides in half) the state. This river runs south to Long Island Sound in the Atlantic Ocean. Farmers grow vegetables and tobacco along the river valley. In colonial times, Connecticut's forests supplied the shipbuilding industry. More than half the state is still forested, but few trees are large enough to be used as timber today.

Almost everyone in Connecticut lives in or near a city. But, there are many small towns scattered throughout the rolling hills. There's little farming, less lumbering, and practically no mining. Even fishing doesn't bring in much money. How does Connecticut manage? It manufactures anything and everything: nails, helicopters, tools, weapons, clocks, and even submarines. If something can be made, Connecticut can make it.

Connecticut has many waterfalls and fast-running streams. These generate waterpower. At the beginning of the Industrial Revolution, industries needed waterpower and workers. Connecticut had both. Another important business in the state is insurance. More insurance companies are in Hartford, Connecticut's capital, than anywhere else in the country.

In 1783, the existing states met to approve the new Constitution. They couldn't agree on how many representatives from each state should be in the government. Larger states wanted representation based on population so that they would have more representatives than smaller states. Smaller states wanted equal representation, the same number of representatives as larger states, regardless of population. Delegates from Connecticut suggested a compromise: equal representation in the Senate, but representation based on population in Congress. Big and small states agreed. Thanks to Connecticut, the "Constitution State," the Constitution was accepted by all.

Connecticut Connections

Nutmeggers, as residents of Connecticut are called, have been the brains behind many American inventions. Below are two lists. The first is a list of Connecticut inventors and their birth years. The second is a list of patented Connecticut inventions and their patent years.

What is a *patent*? An inventor buys a patent to protect a new invention. In the United States, the inventor buys a patent from the federal government. This patent prevents anyone (other than the inventor) from making, using, or selling that invention without the inventor's permission. In the United States, a patent can last longer than 20 years.

Use an encyclopedia or another resource to match these inventors to their inventions. Write the inventor's corresponding letter next to the matching invention. Check off the names as you go along.

A. George Blickensderfer (b. 1850)   ___ 1791   Steamboat

B. Samuel Colt (b. 1814)   ___ 1809   Weaving straw and silk together to make bonnets (First American woman to receive a patent)

C. John Fitch (b. 1743)   ___ 1836   Repeating pistol (revolver)

D. Charles Goodyear (b. 1800)   ___ 1844   Created *vulcanized* (strengthened) rubber used to make tires and sneakers

E. Robert Hall (c. 1919)*   ___ 1846   Sewing machine

F. Elias Howe (b. 1819)   ___ c. 1889* Football tackling dummy

G. Edwin Land (b. 1909)   ___ 1892   Portable typewriter

H. Mary Kies (c. 1788)*   ___ 1946   Instant (Polaroid®) camera

I. Amos Stagg (b. 1862)   ___ 1962   Semiconductor laser later used in CD players

*Note: "c." stands for the Latin word "circa," which is used when you do not know the exact date of an event. Circa means "about" or "approximately" or "around."

CD-0774 50 States

Comprehension Questions

1. Only two other states are smaller than Connecticut.

   True or false? _____

2. Manufacturing means _____.

   A. machinery
   B. making money
   C. making things
   D. working

3. What is the capital of Connecticut?

   _____

4. In the sentence,
   "Delegates from Connecticut suggested a compromise,"
   the word *compromise* means _____.

   A. an agreement midway between two opposite sides
   B. a decision
   C. favoring the larger side
   D. vote

5. Connecticut covers an area of about 5,500 square miles. The strip of land described in the 1662 charter was about 70 miles wide. It is about 3,000 miles from Connecticut's western border to the Pacific Ocean. How big would Connecticut be today if that land still belonged to the state? Show your calculations.

   _____

State Facts

Nickname: _____
Became a State: _____
State Bird: _____
State Flower: _____
State Tree: _____
Fun Fact: _____

DELAWARE

Who says borders aren't round? Look at Delaware. Delaware's border with Pennsylvania is an *arc* (part of a circle). The Pennsylvania Colony originally included Delaware. In 1704, counties in the eastern Delmarva Peninsula separated from Pennsylvania. These "Low Counties" formed their own colony. To make the new border, they drew a 12-mile circle around the northern Delaware city of New Castle. The top of this circle became the Pennsylvania-Delaware border.

Delaware is a tiny sliver of a state. Only Rhode Island is smaller. Delaware's widest point isn't even 40 miles across. A low, flat plain covers most of the state. Migrating waterbirds flock to Delaware's marshes. Sandy beaches filled with tourists line the coast. Delaware has only two major cities. The capital, Dover, is in central Delaware. The largest city, Wilmington, is in northern Delaware. Both are important financial centers. Being close to other large cities, such as Washington, D.C., Baltimore, Philadelphia, and New York City, is good for Delaware. Delaware makes things, and the big cities buy them.

Delaware is the only state that was claimed by Sweden. "New Sweden" was quickly taken over by the Dutch, then the British. After the American Revolution, tiny Delaware was the first of the original Thirteen Colonies to become a state. With statehood came immigrants: Scottish, Irish, German, French, Italian, and Polish. When the British stopped bringing goods to the United States during the War of 1812, Americans were forced to make these goods themselves. An immigrant named DuPont changed Delaware's history. In 1802, DuPont built a gunpowder mill in Wilmington. Today, the DuPont Chemical Company is one of the biggest chemical companies in the world.

Chemicals and finance are not Delaware's only specialties. Farmers grow soybeans and corn. Fishermen haul in crabs and clams, but the biggest business is poultry (young chickens, called *broilers*). Sussex County is the richest farming area in the country, all because of chickens. The Blue Hen Chicken is even Delaware's state bird— but that's because of its reputation as a fierce fighter, not as a tasty meal!

Delaware's Road to Statehood

Delaware was the first of the original Thirteen Colonies to *ratify* (formally approve) the United States Constitution. Before becoming America's "First State," the Delaware area was claimed by three different nations.

Use an encyclopedia or another resource to answer these questions about Delaware's multicultural history.

1. Long before any European set foot in this state, the Delaware Indians lived along the shores of the Delaware River. The name *Delaware* was given to this tribe by the European newcomers. What name did the Delaware Indians call themselves?

   _____

2. In what year did explorer Henry Hudson sail up the Delaware Bay? _____

   What nationality was Henry Hudson? _____

   For which country was Hudson exploring? _____

3. In 1638, Sweden established the colony of New Sweden in the Delaware area. They named their settlement Fort Christina, in honor of their 12-year-old Swedish Queen. The settlement has changed names since 1638, but still lies on the Christina River. What is the name of this city today? _____

4. This 1638 colony of New Sweden was short-lived. It survived only 17 years. What country captured New Sweden from the Swedes? _____

5. The second European colony did not last long, either. In what year did the British conquer the entire New Netherlands colony, including the Delaware area?

   _____

6. Delaware is sometimes called the "First State." It was the first to ratify the Constitution. On what date did Delaware vote to accept the Constitution?

   _____

7. The flags of four nations fly from New Castle's Court House in Delaware, reflecting Delaware's multicultural history. What are the names of these four nations?

   _____

   _____

   _____

Comprehension Questions

1. Delaware is the 13th state.

   True or false? _____

2. On which side of the state is Delaware's circular border?

   A. east
   B. north
   C. south
   D. west

3. Name two major cities in Delaware.

   _____   _____

4. In the sentence,
   "Migrating waterbirds flock to Delaware's marshes,"
   the word *migrating* means _____.

   A. living together
   B. moving with the change of seasons
   C. swimming in a group
   D. traveling for fun

5. Delaware is on the Delmarva Peninsula. Delaware shares this peninsula with Maryland to the west, and Virginia to the south. Why do you think this peninsula is called the Delmarva Peninsula?

   _____

   _____

   _____

   _____

   _____

DELAWARE

DISTRICT OF COLUMBIA

Look! There's Thomas Jefferson, author of the Declaration of Independence. And isn't that Franklin D. Roosevelt, the only president to be elected four times? That thoughtful-looking man must be Abraham Lincoln, leader of the country during the Civil War. There's Teddy Roosevelt . . . and John F. Kennedy . . . and First Lady Eleanor Roosevelt. Is this time-travel? No. It's Washington, D.C.

These American politicians are long gone, but their bronze and marble images live on. Washington is full of memorials and monuments to famous people and events. Climb the 897 steps to the top of the Washington Monument. Run your fingers along the names of thousands of heroic Vietnam War Veterans, or view the statues at the Korean War Veterans Memorial. Visit Ford's Theatre, where President Lincoln was assassinated. Get lost in the Library of Congress, the world's largest library. Check out the amazing Smithsonian Institute. The many Smithsonian museums and buildings are guaranteed to feed your brain cells!

Washington, D.C. has been the capital of the United States since 1800. Every American president except George Washington has lived in this city. Washington D.C. is located along the Potomac River, between Maryland and Virginia. It is a planned city. George Washington selected the location. The region is called the District of Columbia (D.C.) in honor of Christopher Columbus. Washington, D.C. is not a state. It is under direct control of the federal government. The city of Washington covers the entire D.C. area. Washington's suburbs extend into neighboring states.

All three branches of American government are based in these 68 square miles. The President lives in the White House on Pennsylvania Avenue. Minutes away, on Capitol Hill, is the United States Capitol Building. This is where senators and members of Congress meet to pass laws that affect you, your family, and the entire country. The Supreme Court is nearby. The Supreme Court Justices meet here to determine if American laws are constitutional—that means, if they obey the United States Constitution.

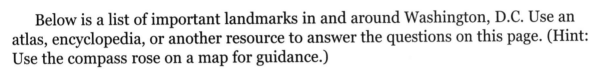

Finding Your Way through the Nation's Capital

Washington, D.C., the nation's capital, was carefully planned out before being built. The city is centered around Capitol Hill. Most government offices, memorials, and monuments are west of the Capitol building. Some important government sites are located across the Potomac River, in nearby Arlington, Virginia.

Below is a list of important landmarks in and around Washington, D.C. Use an atlas, encyclopedia, or another resource to answer the questions on this page. (Hint: Use the compass rose on a map for guidance.)

Arlington National Cemetery
The White House
John F. Kennedy Center for the Performing Arts
Library of Congress
Lincoln Memorial
The Pentagon

Theodore Roosevelt Memorial
Thomas Jefferson Memorial
United States Capitol
Vietnam War Veterans Memorial
Washington Monument
Korean War Veterans Memorial

Using the compass rose on the map for guidance, answer the following questions:

1. What two buildings are located east of the Washington Monument?

_____

2. What building is located on an island in the Potomac River?

_____

3. What two landmarks are located in the state of Virginia?

_____

4. What landmark is found closest to the Jefferson Memorial?

_____

5. What two landmarks are found directly south of the White House?

_____

6. What two memorials are found closest to the Lincoln Memorial?

_____

_____

7. This landmark is found west of the reflecting pool, next to the Potomac River.

_____

DISTRICT OF COLUMBIA

Comprehension Questions

1. Washington, D.C., shares a border with the state of Maryland.

   True or false? _____

2. Which of the following Washington, D.C., statues is NOT of a United States President?

   A. J. Kennedy
   B. E. Roosevelt
   C. F. Roosevelt
   D. T. Roosevelt

3. The United States declared independence from Britain in 1776. How many years passed before Washington, D.C., became the nation's capital?

   _____

4. In the sentence,
   "Visit Ford's Theatre, where President Lincoln was assassinated,"
   the word *assassinated* means _____.

   A. coronated
   B. elected
   C. murdered
   D. buried

5. James Smithson was a British scientist who had never set foot on American soil. When Smithson died in 1829, he left his entire fortune to the United States of America. In his will, Smithson stated that the United States could only use this money for the "increase and diffusion (spreading) of knowledge." The Smithsonian Institute was created from this money. What sort of knowledge do you think Smithson had in mind? Give some examples.

   _____

   _____

   _____

   _____

DISTRICT OF COLUMBIA

State Facts

Nickname: _____

Became a State: _____

State Bird: _____

State Flower: _____

State Tree: _____

Fun Fact: _____

FLORIDA

Look at the southeastern corner of a map of the United States. No other state looks like this one. The top of Florida (the Panhandle) is so wide it falls into two time zones. The bottom (the peninsula) dangles 450 miles into the ocean. This peninsula separates the Gulf of Mexico from the Atlantic Ocean. If you're looking for mountains, or even hills, you're out of luck. On the other hand, if you dream of warm temperatures, sunny days, ocean beaches, and fresh oranges, this is the place for you.

Except for the hilly northwest, most of Florida is low and flat. Water is always close by. Sandbars and coral reefs run along the Atlantic Coast. The Florida Keys are islands that reach southwest into the Gulf of Mexico. Atlantic hurricanes occasionally bring heavy rainfall and flooding. Thousands of freshwater lakes cover northern and central Florida. Lake Okeechobee, in the south, is one of the largest lakes in the country. The southern tip of Florida is a swamp. Drained swamp land throughout Florida has allowed crops to be planted and cities to be built.

Florida bounced back and forth between Spain and Britain for 300 years before becoming part of the United States in 1821. Florida's Seminole Indians fought hard against settlement, but most were eventually forced to move west. Americans poured into the state. They drained the soggy land. They mined for phosphate, which is used in fertilizer. They planted citrus crops such as oranges and grapefruits, then added tomatoes. They fished the oceans and they enjoyed the sun. These things haven't changed.

People still come to Florida from other places. Older people retire to Florida's warmth. Caribbean refugees, mainly from nearby Cuba, arrive looking for a better life. Electronics experts appear, eager to be part of Cape Canaveral's Space Program. For every person who lives in Florida, twice as many people come to visit every year. There's nothing like Walt Disney World® in Orlando to entertain tourists. The same thing that attracted people to Florida years ago still exists. Florida is, indeed, the "Sunshine State."

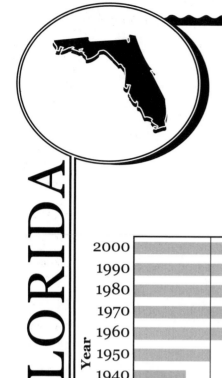

FLORIDA

Moving to Florida?

People move to Florida for many different reasons. Some people move to the "Sunshine State" to enjoy the warm weather. Other people move to Florida from nearby countries, looking for a better life. Whatever the reason, Florida is one of the fastest growing states in the country. Use the chart below to answer the following questions about Florida's population. Populations are rounded to the nearest million or fraction of one million. [Hint: Your answers will be *approximate* (not exact).]

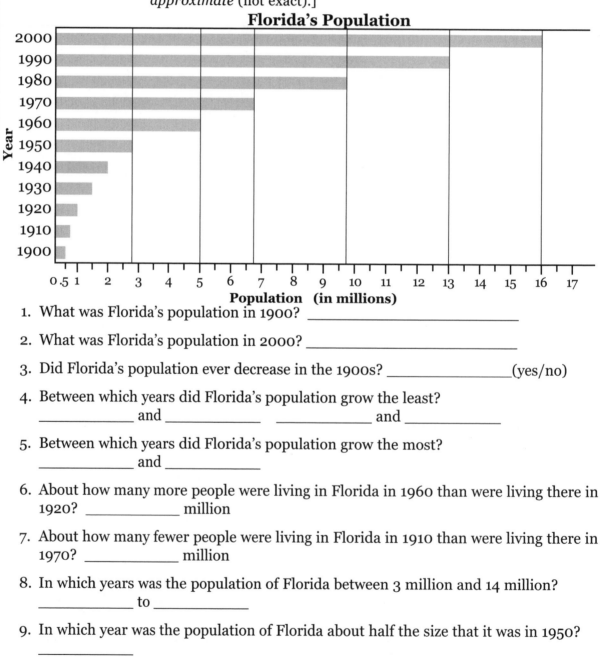

Florida's Population

1. What was Florida's population in 1900? _____

2. What was Florida's population in 2000? _____

3. Did Florida's population ever decrease in the 1900s? _____(yes/no)

4. Between which years did Florida's population grow the least?
   _____ and _____   _____ and _____

5. Between which years did Florida's population grow the most?
   _____ and _____

6. About how many more people were living in Florida in 1960 than were living there in 1920? _____ million

7. About how many fewer people were living in Florida in 1910 than were living there in 1970? _____ million

8. In which years was the population of Florida between 3 million and 14 million?
   _____ to _____

9. In which year was the population of Florida about half the size that it was in 1950?
   _____

10. In which year was the population of Florida more than three times the size that it was in 1960? _____

Comprehension Questions

1. Florida was once under Spanish rule.

   True or false? _____

2. Phosphate rock is used in which of the following products?

   A. citrus
   B. electronics
   C. fertilizer
   D. tourism

3. Florida was home to what Native American tribe?

   _____

4. In the sentence,
   "Caribbean refugees, mainly from nearby Cuba, arrive looking for a better life,"
   the word *refugees* means _____.

   A. natives
   B. people on vacation
   C. people seeking safety
   D. visitors

5. The northwestern part of Florida is called a *Panhandle*. This word is used in geography to describe a particular shape of land. What do you think that shape is? Why do we use that word to describe that part of Florida?

   _____

   _____

   _____

   _____

   _____

FLORIDA

GEORGIA

Nickname: _____
Became a State: _____
State Bird: _____
State Flower: _____
State Tree: _____
Fun Fact: _____

Why is Georgia called the "Empire State of the South?" Georgia is definitely a southern state. Head any further south and you end up in Florida. Georgia is also one of the largest states east of the Mississippi River. It is even bigger than New York, the original "Empire State," and Georgia leads the South in industry and manufacturing.

Georgia didn't start out as an empire. It was originally created as a colony for England's poor. In 1732, British *philanthropists* (people wanting to help other people) received permission to create a new colony. It was named Georgia, for King George II of England. Many of the first settlers came to Georgia with help from these philanthropists. Georgia was the last of the original Thirteen Colonies. In 1788, Georgia became the fourth state. Georgia's cotton farms grew larger, cotton plantation owners grew richer, and Georgia was on its way to becoming an empire.

Georgia has many different "faces." Mountains run through northern Georgia. Central Georgia is covered in rolling hills. Flat, coastal plains lie in the south. Georgia has a variety of natural resources, too. Mining produces marble, granite, and *kaolin* (white clay used to make china). Georgia's towering pine trees are used to make paper. Major rivers flow throughout the state. Ocean beaches are crowded with tourists. Chickens and eggs are sold by the millions. Georgia is number one in the production of peanuts. Georgia is also a leader in pecans, tobacco, and peaches. And don't forget cotton. Georgia's huge clothing and carpet industries need all the cotton they can get.

After the Civil War, Georgia rebuilt itself. It is home to military bases, food processing plants, and technology companies. The ocean port of Savannah transports goods in and out of the South. Atlanta, Georgia's capital, is a financial giant. Those philanthropists had no idea how great a state their colony would become!

Mapping Georgia's Capital Cities

Since Georgia was first colonized in 1733, it has had five different capitals. These capitals are listed below. After carefully reading each clue, label the map to show where these capitals are located. Label the capitals using the corresponding letters. Use an atlas if necessary.

A. Savannah
1733—1786

Savannah is the oldest settlement in Georgia. It lies at the mouth of the Savannah River. Interstates 16 and 95 meet just outside Savannah.

B. Augusta
1786—1796

Augusta is the second oldest city in Georgia. It was named for England's Princess of Wales. Georgians were moving away from the Atlantic coast, so the capital moved, too. Augusta lies midway along the Savannah River. Interstate 20 crosses through Augusta from neighboring South Carolina.

C. Louisville
1796—1807

Louisville was Georgia's first planned capital city. Louisville was named in honor of King Louis XVI of France for his country's help during the American Revolution. It lies south of Augusta, midway between Interstates 20 and 16.

D. Milledgeville
1807—1868

As settlers moved further inland, so did the capital. Milledgeville was named for John Milledge, Governor of Georgia in 1806. Milledgeville is in the geographic center of the state. It lies between Interstate 20 and the west end of Interstate 16.

E. Atlanta
1868—present

The Chattahoochee River runs around the western edge of Atlanta. Interstates 85, 75, and 20 meet here. Atlanta started off as the final stop on a railroad line. It was burned to the ground during the Civil War, but is now the financial capital of the South.

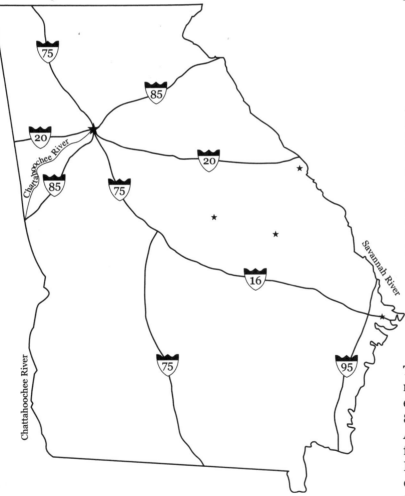

Comprehension Questions

GEORGIA

1. The city of Savannah is located near the ocean.

   True or false? _____

2. Which of the following geographical features is NOT found in Georgia?

   A. Deserts
   B. Mountains
   C. Plains
   D. Rivers

3. Name four important crops grown in Georgia.

   _____

   _____

   _____

   _____

4. In the sentence,
   "Georgia's towering pine trees are used to make paper,"
   the word *towering* means _____.

   A. bark-covered
   B. many
   C. tall
   D. wide

5. Eli Whitney invented the cotton gin in Savannah, Georgia, in 1793. This machine removed the cotton seeds from the cotton fiber quickly and easily. With the cotton gin, farmers were able to grow more cotton on their plantations. How do you think the invention of the cotton gin affected life in Georgia?

   _____

   _____

   _____

State Facts

Nickname: _____
Became a State: _____
State Bird: _____
State Flower: _____
State Tree: _____
Fun Fact: _____

HAWAII

America's only state that is an island chain, Hawaii, lies far from the continental United States in the Pacific Ocean. Hawaii is the nation's youngest state; it joined the Union in 1959. Hawaii is also the world's longest island chain; it is actually a string of 132 islands that formed when volcanoes erupted along the ocean floor. The smaller islands are composed of coral, sand, rock, or lava. Their volcanoes have been long since worn away by water. The eight larger southeastern islands are the ones that we usually think of when we refer to Hawaii. These islands remain high above sea level, and volcanoes, some still active, are common. The climate is *tropical* (humid and mild all year round, with little temperature change between night and day).

Polynesians first came to Hawaii over 2,000 years ago. Until the British explorer James Cook came ashore in 1778, Europeans knew little of the islands. After Cook's visit, the islands were united under a single Hawaiian king. King Kamehameha I's children and their descendants ruled for nearly a century. First, foreigners arrived as missionaries to convert the native people to Christianity. Then, foreigners came as whalers on whaling ships. Workers on sugar cane and pineapple plantations followed. By 1900, a revolution had toppled the royal monarchy and Hawaii became a territory of the United States.

Of the main islands, the southernmost island is by far the largest. This island is also called Hawaii. The world's most massive volcano, Mauna Kea, and most active volcano, Mauna Loa, are found on this island. Hawaii is known locally as "Big Island" for its great size. The seven other main islands are Maui, uninhabited Kahoolawe, pineapple-rich Lanai, Molokai, Oahu (home to more than 70% of the island's population, and location of the capital, Honolulu), Kauai, and the privately owned Niihau.

Hawaii is the only state that has an official language other than English. This state, so many miles away from the rest of the country, calls itself the "Aloha State." In the Hawaiian language, *Aloha* means "love," and is used to greet and bid farewell.

H...A...W...A...I...I

Learn more about the state of Hawaii. Use a dictionary, encyclopedia, or atlas to help you fill in the blanks in the sentences below. Each of the missing words starts with the corresponding letter in the name Hawaii.

H   Hawaii is in the H __ __ __ __ __ __ - __ __ __ __ __ __ __ __ __ Time Zone, which is two hours behind California (Pacific Time Zone), and five hours behind New York (Eastern Time Zone). Since Hawaii observes standard time year round, Hawaii is an additional hour behind the mainland during daylight-saving time.

A   An a __ __ __ __ __ __ __ __ __ __ __ is a group of islands spread over a large area of water. The Hawaiian Islands are an example of such a group.

W   Mount W __ __ __ __ __ __ __ __, on the lush island of Kauai, is the wettest place in the world. Rainfall there averages about 460 inches (38 feet!) in a single year.

A   The United States entered World War II after an attack on its Naval Base at Pearl Harbor, in Oahu's Mamala Bay, on December 7, 1941. The USS A __ __ __ __ __ __ warship was sunk in that attack.

I   The last severe hurricane to hit Hawaii was Hurricane I __ __ __ __ in 1982, when flooding caused devastating damage to the island of Kauai.

I   The Hawaiian Kingdom's last monarchs, King Kalakaua and his sister Queen Liliuokalani, lived in the I __ __ __ __ __ Palace in Honolulu. This is the only building in the United States that was originally built for royalty.

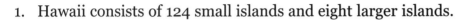

Comprehension Questions

1. Hawaii consists of 124 small islands and eight larger islands.

   True or false? _____

2. Which of the following is NOT the name of one of the main Hawaiian islands?

   A. Kahoolawe
   B. Kamehameha
   C. Oahu
   D. Niihau

3. What was explorer James Cook's nationality?

   _____

4. In the sentence,
   "The smaller islands are composed of coral, sand, rock, or lava,"
   the word *composed* means _____.

   A. covered with
   B. floating in
   C. made up of
   D. stacked on top of

5. The volcanoes in Hawaii do not explode upward and outward like Washington's Mount St. Helens. They do not have high, steep peaks. Hawaii's volcanoes are known as shield volcanoes. The lava in these volcanoes is hotter and thinner, and flows more easily. Instead of exploding, it overflows, spilling and spreading over the entire mountainside. How do you think this type of lava flow has affected the shape of the Hawaiian mountains?

   _____

   _____

   _____

   _____

HAWAII

State Facts

Nickname: _____

Became a State: _____

State Bird: _____

State Flower: _____

State Tree: _____

Fun Fact: _____

IDAHO

To some people, Idaho represents the wild west: Hells Canyon, Horsethief Reservoir, Seven Devils Mountains, and . . . potatoes? Yes, potatoes. If you are eating potato chips, french fries, or mashed potatoes, chances are that the potatoes came from the state of Idaho.

Idaho is a rugged state. Its mountains are jagged and difficult to cross. Early travelers avoided Idaho's Rockies. They followed the Oregon Trail along the Snake River. This river runs across southern Idaho and up the western border into Washington State. Idaho's southern plateau was created thousands of years ago when layers of lava covered the plain. The soil is fertile and perfect for potatoes, wheat, barley, and other crops.

Idaho is rich in water. Thousands of lakes lie in the forested mountains. Mineral springs bubble up from the ground. Rivers flow across the state. Lewiston, a city on the Snake River, is Idaho's doorway to the Pacific Ocean. The ocean is 500 miles away, but the Snake-Columbia River System connects Idaho to the Pacific. The moist ocean air affects Idaho's weather. Idaho has warmer winters and cooler summers than its neighbors to the east.

In 1805, President Thomas Jefferson sent Meriwether Lewis and William Clark on an expedition to the Pacific Ocean. The success of this expedition brought the first settlers to Idaho. More passed through on their way to the California goldfields in 1849. But the Shoshone, Nez Perce, and other Native American tribes had Idaho practically all to themselves until the 1860s. Gold, then silver and lead, brought more settlers. Cattle ranchers followed. The government forced the Native Americans onto reservations. In 1890, Idaho became a state.

Many modern Idahoans still make a living from the land. Miners dig for silver, lead, and phosphate rock. Farmers herd cattle and grow crops. Loggers chop pine trees. Other people work to *process* (change) these products. They work in fertilizer factories, paper mills, and food processing plants. Boise, the capital, is home to electronics and computer companies.

Idaho's Natural Resources

Idaho is rich in natural resources. Listed in the word bank below are important Idahoan resources. Find and circle each of these words in the Idaho Resources Puzzle, including the labels Agriculture, Forestry, and Mining. (Hint: Names with more than one word will be found together in the puzzle.)

Word Bank

Agriculture
barley
beef
cheese
dairy
hay
milk
oats
onions
peas
potatoes
sheep
sugar beets
wheat

Forestry
cedar
fir
lumber
paper
pine

Mining
antimony
copper
feldspar
gold
lead
molybdenum
perlite
phosphate
quartz
silver
tungsten
vanadium
zinc

Idaho Resources

```
F I R G Z K W A X S O X S L O D B I T U
E W F Z Y E L D G M P R L T U N A E Q B
H M L F H I A F U R A J T P C M I I E A
A S X A S E A N E P I U O U E H B O R F
Y T U S X A E T S S Q C A R N R E E N Y
A I T J I D A D E U D R U N E G L E R S
T A B X B H L O M A N P Z L T S S I S W
O E J Y P E T M N M A T K S T I M T T E
S Q L S F A U T A N R M T G I U M R E E
B O O N T I Z P W A F A F R F L R O Y N
M H S O D Y U A U L E W O J W S V E N V
P J P A E R E Q N H J L R R Q M H E S Y
X N N L E G R K W H C Q E C D Y P E R M
E A R P N G G U P R E E S Q E X M T E Q
V A P I D P E A S J D H T I D K B I B P
B O N Q R K I H A X A Y R C I A E Q J P
C I C E M I L K X Z R V Y M H F T V V X
M T P Z P I Y T R E I D Z I N C L E A D
I A G O L D U F L E V S L Y P F P I N E
P S U G A R B E E T S Z Q B O C L G U I
```

Idaho's nickname reflects this abundance of natural resources, especially those found underground. In the top eight horizontal rows, circle the first unused letter. These letters, in order, will spell Idaho's nickname.

_____ _____ _____   _____ _____ _____ _____

Comprehension Questions

1. The Oregon Trail passed through Idaho.

   True or false? _____

2. Which of these crops is NOT grown in Idaho?

   A. barley
   B. citrus
   C. potatoes
   D. wheat

3. Name two Native American tribes found in Idaho.

   _____

   _____

4. In the sentence,
   "The moist ocean air affects Idaho's weather,"
   the word *moist* means _____.

   A. cold
   B. damp
   C. strong
   D. windy

5. Lewiston is a city on the Snake River. It was the first capital of the Idaho Territory. Members of the 1805 Lewis and Clark Expedition camped in Lewiston during their trip to the Pacific Ocean. How do you think Lewiston got its name?

   _____

   _____

   _____

   _____

IDAHO

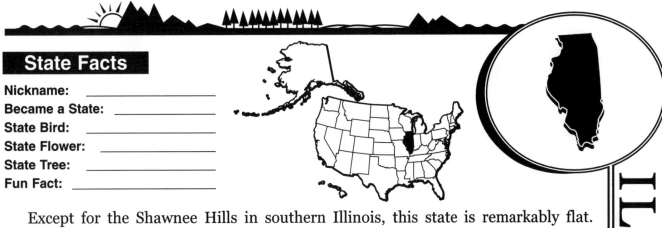

State Facts

Nickname: _____

Became a State: _____

State Bird: _____

State Flower: _____

State Tree: _____

Fun Fact: _____

ILLINOIS

Except for the Shawnee Hills in southern Illinois, this state is remarkably flat. However, rising up from the level prairie is one of the world's tallest buildings, Chicago's Sears Tower. Chicago is the largest city in Illinois. It is the third largest city in the country. And if it weren't for Illinoisan Nathaniel Pope, Chicago would actually be in the state of Wisconsin.

Illinois became a state in 1818. The Mississippi River formed the western border with Missouri and Iowa. The Ohio River formed the southern border with Kentucky. The eastern border with Indiana had already been set two years earlier. But the northern border was a problem. It extended from the southern tip of Lake Michigan straight west to the Mississippi River. Pope persuaded Congress to include an extra 60-mile strip of land across the northern border of the new state; therefore, Chicago became part of Illinois.

It's not surprising that the "Prairie State" has become the transportation center of the country. To the east lies Lake Michigan, one of the Great Lakes. This leads to the Atlantic Ocean. To the west, it has the Mississippi River. This runs into the Gulf of Mexico. Rivers and canals within Illinois connect these two water systems. Illinois has more roads and railroad tracks than almost any other state. Chicago's O'Hare airport is one of the busiest in the nation.

Illinois needs these transportation facilities. It has a lot to move. Farms cover three-fourths of the state. Soybeans, corn, wheat, and apples grow well on the fertile prairie soil. Farmers raise hogs and beef and dairy cattle. Miners dig for coal. The Chicago area is a major manufacturing center for machinery and food processing. Business travelers from all over the country come to Chicago to attend conferences. Tourists head for Abraham Lincoln historical sites in Illinois' capital, Springfield.

Illinois' cold winters, hot summers and frequent tornadoes didn't scare off 19th-century European immigrants. They don't seem to be a problem for the more than 12 million people who call Illinois home.

Touring Illinois

Use an atlas or an encyclopedia to locate the Illinois towns and cities listed below. Match these cities with the letters shown on the map. Write the correct letter next to each city name.

ILLINOIS

E   A   D

B

C

F

G

____ **Springfield**
This city has been the capital of Illinois since 1839. The 16th President, Abraham Lincoln, lived there for 24 years. He was married and buried there.

____ **Vandalia**
This city was Illinois' first state capital.

____ **Bloomington**
This is where Abraham Lincoln gave his famous "Lost Speech" against slavery. This speech was "lost" because the reporters who attended the convention were so excited by Lincoln's words that they forgot to take notes.

____ **Cairo**
The states of Illinois, Missouri, and Kentucky meet at Cairo, where the Ohio River meets the Mississippi River. Cairo was named for the Egyptian city of the same name. The southern tip of Illinois is sometimes called "Little Egypt."

____ **Chicago**
The Great Chicago Fire of 1871 left almost 100,000 people homeless. Chicago soon rebuilt itself, and in 1893 it hosted the successful Chicago World's Fair. One of the most popular attractions at the fair was the Ferris Wheel, invented for the fair by George Ferris.

____ **De Kalb**
Joseph Glidden, from De Kalb, Illinois, invented barbed wire in 1873. Barbed wire changed life in the American West. Huge herds of cattle could now be fenced in, thus ending the wandering life of the cowboy.

____ **Dixon**
Ronald Reagan, the 40th President, grew up in Dixon. There, he prepared for his careers as an actor and a politician by performing in school plays and joining the Student Council.

Comprehension Questions

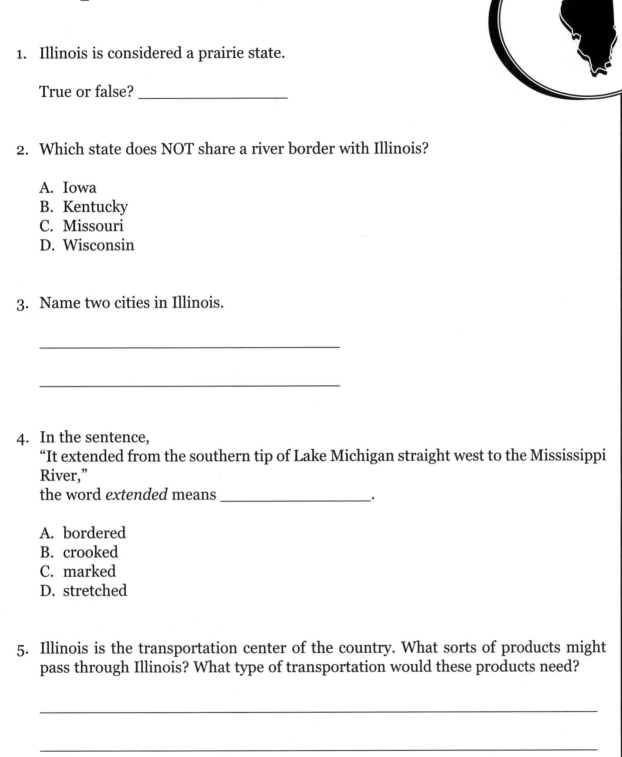

1. Illinois is considered a prairie state.

    True or false? _____

2. Which state does NOT share a river border with Illinois?

    A. Iowa
    B. Kentucky
    C. Missouri
    D. Wisconsin

3. Name two cities in Illinois.

    _____

    _____

4. In the sentence,
    "It extended from the southern tip of Lake Michigan straight west to the Mississippi River,"
    the word *extended* means _____.

    A. bordered
    B. crooked
    C. marked
    D. stretched

5. Illinois is the transportation center of the country. What sorts of products might pass through Illinois? What type of transportation would these products need?

    _____

    _____

    _____

    _____

ILLINOIS

INDIANA

State Facts

Nickname: _____
Became a State: _____
State Bird: _____
State Flower: _____
State Tree: _____
Fun Fact: _____

Indiana means "Land of the Indians." But most of Indiana's Native Americans actually came from somewhere else. When 17th-century French fur traders arrived in the Indiana area, they found few Native Americans living there. But as white settlers filled up the land east of Indiana, Native Americans were pushed west into the Indiana region. First, Indiana became a territory. Then, in 1816, it became a state. More white settlers came to Indiana. One by one, the Indian tribes had to sign treaties giving up this new land, too. Today, less than one percent of Indiana's population is Native American.

Indiana is a small state compared to its bigger western neighbors. It stretches south from Lake Michigan down to the Ohio River. If you look at a map, you'll see that most roads pass through the center of the state. That's where you'll find Indianapolis, Indiana's capital and largest city. One of the first major roads ever built in the United States runs right through this city. Today, this early road is only one of many highways that *intersect* (go through) the capital. Roads from Indianapolis stretch out in all directions like long spider legs. These roads pass through Indiana's flat central plain. Drive by and you'll see fields of corn and soybeans, hog farms, and grazing cattle. Some of the roads leaving Indianapolis head far north to steel mills and oil refineries. Other roads head south to coal mines in the hills, valleys, and caves near the Ohio River. A few roads take you into Amish settlements. Here, Amish farmers drive horse-drawn buggies instead of cars.

Agriculture has always been important to Indiana. Farms cover two-thirds of the state. But manufacturing is even more important: steel, aluminum, electronics, and anything else to do with cars. The first gasoline-powered car was invented over a century ago in Kokomo, Indiana. Since then, cars have become a big part of Indiana's economy. The famous Indianapolis 500 car race has been held in Indianapolis since 1911. Even the Indiana state motto reflects this love for cars: "The Crossroads of America."

Mapping Your Own Indy 500

The Indianapolis 500 is a famous car race held in Indianapolis every year. Cars race 200 times around a two and one-half mile oval track, for a total distance of 500 miles. You and some other drivers decide to drive race cars through the state instead. Look at the map below. Indianapolis is at the center. A road leads to each of eight cities. The mileage between the different cities is written on the map. To get the correct answers, always start and end in Indianapolis, and find the shortest possible route.

Car #1: Robert wants to check out antique cars at the Studebaker National Museum in South Bend, one of Indiana's largest cities. He also wants to visit Johnny Appleseed's grave in Indiana's second largest city, Fort Wayne. How many miles long will Robert's trip be?

_____

Car #2: Kara wants to drive to Terre Haute, a city on the Wabash River. She would also like to visit Fountain City, a stop on the Underground Railroad. Before the Civil War, thousands of southern slaves used the Underground Railroad to escape to freedom in Canada. How many miles long will Kara's trip be?

_____

What route did she take?   _____
_____
_____

Car #3: You want to see Vincennes, Indiana's first permanent settlement. Then, you want to explore some of the largest underground caves: the Wyandotte Caves near Wyandotte. How many miles long will your trip be? _____

Car #4: Alonzo wants to drive to the Falls of the Ohio State Park, near Clarksville, to see 400-million-year-old fossils. Then, he's going to visit Tippecanoe Battlefield in Battle Ground, where Governor William Harrison, who later became the ninth U.S. President, led troops against Shawnee Chief Tecumseh in 1811. How many miles long will Alonzo's trip be? _____

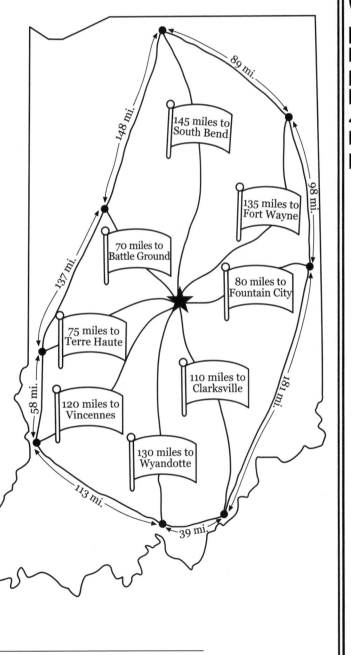

INDIANA

Comprehension Questions

INDIANA

1. Part of Indiana lies on Lake Superior, one of the Great Lakes.

   True or false? _____

2. When did Indiana become a state?

   A. 1816
   B. 1875
   C. 1894
   D. 1911

3. Name an important river that runs along Indiana's southern border.

   _____

4. In the sentence,
   "One by one, the Indian tribes had to sign treaties giving up this new land, too,"
   the word *treaties* means _____.

   A. agreements
   B. books
   C. papers
   D. signatures

5. Why do you think Indianapolis was chosen as the capital of Indiana?

   _____

   _____

   _____

   _____

   _____

   _____

   _____

Nickname: _____

Became a State: _____

State Bird: _____

State Flower: _____

State Tree: _____

Fun Fact: _____

IOWA

What do food, corn, hogs, soybeans, cows, and Iowa have in common? They are all four-letter words, with an *o* as the second letter. But there's another connection. Almost one-tenth of all the food we eat comes from Iowa! This state is the nation's leader in corn and hog production. It is a major producer of soybeans, and it raises a huge number of dairy and beef cattle. Iowa provides food for people and livestock all over the world.

If you were a bird flying high above Iowa, what would you see? An enormous checkerboard! The squares on this checkerboard are fields of crops. These fields are divided by roads, rivers, and more fields. Ice Age glaciers left Iowa flat and fertile. Almost all the land in the state is farmland. In the past, most Iowans worked on farms. Today, that has changed. Agriculture is still extremely important, but fewer people work directly on the land.

Now, more Iowans live in cities than on farms. They find jobs at food processing plants, creating breakfast cereals. They manufacture tractors and other farm machinery. They make washing machines and refrigerators. They work for insurance companies in cities such as Des Moines, the state capital. But agriculture still rules.

Iowa is the only state bordered by both the Missouri and Mississippi Rivers, the two longest rivers in the country. The Missouri River (and its tributary, the Big Sioux River) separates Iowa from South Dakota and Nebraska. The Mississippi River separates Iowa from Wisconsin and Illinois. Barges travel up and down these rivers. Many smaller rivers flow throughout the state. Flooding can be a problem, but at least Iowa doesn't have to worry about running out of water!

Hogs or Cows?

The graph below shows the prices that Iowa farmers received for their hogs and beef cattle. The prices are shown in ten-year increments from 1910 to 2000. The price is shown as dollars per hundred pounds of animal weight. Use the graph to answer the questions about the livestock. The solid line shows the price of hogs. The dotted line shows the price of beef cattle.

IOWA

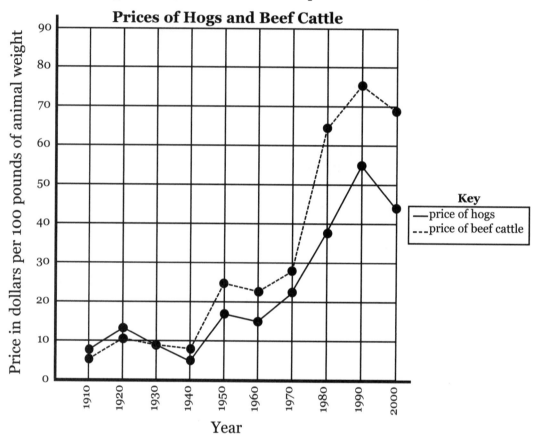

Prices of Hogs and Beef Cattle

Price in dollars per 100 pounds of animal weight

Year

Key
— price of hogs
--- price of beef cattle

1. In which years was the price of hogs greater than the price of cattle? _____

2. In which years was the price of hogs less than the price of cattle? _____

3. In which years were the prices of hogs and cattle the same? _____

4. In 1910, which type of livestock sold at a higher price? _____

5. In 1950, which type of livestock sold at a lower price? _____

6. In 1980, which livestock sold at a higher price? _____

7. In which year did cattle reach its *peak* (highest) price? What was it? _____

8. In which year did cattle reach its lowest price? What was it? _____

9. In which year did hogs reach their peak price? What was it? _____

10. In which year did hogs reach their lowest price? What was it? _____

Comprehension Questions

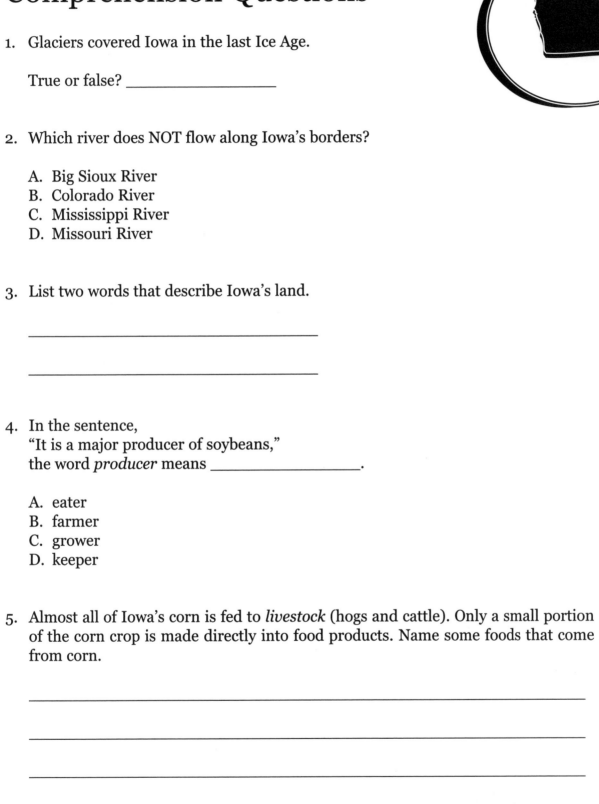

1. Glaciers covered Iowa in the last Ice Age.

   True or false? _____

2. Which river does NOT flow along Iowa's borders?

   A. Big Sioux River
   B. Colorado River
   C. Mississippi River
   D. Missouri River

3. List two words that describe Iowa's land.

   _____

   _____

4. In the sentence,
   "It is a major producer of soybeans,"
   the word *producer* means _____.

   A. eater
   B. farmer
   C. grower
   D. keeper

5. Almost all of Iowa's corn is fed to *livestock* (hogs and cattle). Only a small portion of the corn crop is made directly into food products. Name some foods that come from corn.

   _____

   _____

   _____

   _____

IOWA

State Facts

Nickname: _____
Became a State: _____
State Bird: _____
State Flower: _____
State Tree: _____
Fun Fact: _____

What state lies smack-dab in the middle of the country? Kansas. This state is almost a perfect rectangle. Its borders have been carved right out of the prairie, except for the Missouri River in the northeast.

Long before settlers arrived, Native Americans built a network of trails throughout the state. Traders traveled the Santa Fe Trail from Missouri to New Mexico. Prospectors followed the Oregon Trail to California gold mines. But it was the Chisholm Trail that put Wichita (Kansas' largest city) on the map. To the south, Texas was overflowing with cattle. To the north, people wanted meat. Cowboys herded their cattle along the Chisholm Trail to Kansas towns such as Abilene and Wichita. The cattle were loaded onto railway cars and shipped north. Eventually, Texas got its own railroad, and cowboys stopped driving along the Chisholm Trail. Even so, Kansas continued to grow.

Kansas is now known as the Sunflower State, and its highest point is Mount Sunflower, which rises 4,039 feet about sea level. Grazing herds of cattle and golden fields of wheat cover the land. Salt, oil and natural gas lie under the flat prairie soil. Wichita is a leader in the airplane industry. Food processing and machinery manufacturing is important in many towns, including the capital, Topeka.

The Kansas prairie was once the hunting grounds for the Plains Indians. Today, most of the Native American tribes and buffalo are gone. Only the Iowa, Kickapoo, Potawatomi, Sak, and Fox tribes remain on reservations in the state. Severe droughts have taught Kansans the importance of conserving their natural resources. Kansas has few lakes, so artificial lakes were created to hold water. Farmers have adjusted their planting and plowing habits to help keep their soil healthy. Tornadoes, hail storms, and dust storms frequently attack Kansas. But occasional bad weather doesn't stop the "Breadbasket of America" from continuously producing record amounts of wheat.

Kansas Cattle Towns

You are an 1880s cattle buyer in Dodge City, Kansas. You are going to travel by horse throughout the state to buy cattle. You have a list of Kansas towns to visit, but the list has been torn in half. It doesn't show the names of the towns, but it still shows the compass direction and distance you must travel between each town.

The starting point, Dodge City, is in southwestern Kansas. It is marked with an **X**. Go to new towns by moving the given number of squares in the listed direction from the last town you visited. Write each town's name in the spaces provided near that instruction. You will visit all the towns at least once. The first stop after Dodge City has been done for you. When you are finished, write the boxed letters in order in the blanks below to spell out another name for 19th-century Dodge City.

Start at Dodge City
1. Go E 8, N 1
Y a t e s C e n t e r

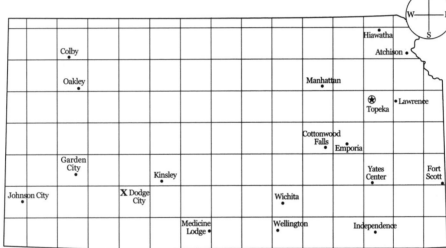

2. Go N 4
_ _ _ _ _ ☐ _

3. Go S 2
_ _ _ ☐ _ _

---

4. Go E 1 _ _ ☐ _ _ _ _ _   5. Go N 2 _ _ _ _ ☐ _ _ _

6. Go W 11 ☐ _ _ _ _   7. Go S 1 _ _ ☐ _ ☐ _   8. Go S 3 _ _ _ ☐☐ _ _ _ _ _

9. Go E 12 _ _ _ _ ☐ _ _ ☐ _   10. Go W 9 _ _ _ _ ☐ _ _

11. Go E 4, S 1 _ ☐ _ _ _ ☐ _   12. Go S 1 _ _ _ _ _ _ _ ☐ _ _

13. Go W 3 _ _ _ _ _ _ ☐ _ _ _ ☐   14. Go W 6, N 1 _ _ _ _ _ _ _ ☐☐☐☐

15. Go E 12, S 1 ☐☐ _ _ _ _ _ _ _ _ _   16. Go N 4 _ _ _ _ _ ☐

17. Go N 1, W 2 ☐ _ _ _ _ _ _ _ _   18. Go S2, E 1 ☐ _ _ _ ☐☐ _

19. Go W 1   ☐ _ _ _ _ _ _ _ _ _ ☐ _ _ _

_ _ _ _ _   _ _ _ _ _ _ _ _ _ _ _

_ _ _ _ _

Comprehension Questions

1. Most of Kansas' borders are marked by rivers.

   True or false? _____

2. The Chisholm Trail ended in Kansas. Where did it start?

   A. California
   B. Missouri
   C. New Mexico
   D. Texas

3. What is the name of the largest city in Kansas?

   _____

4. In the sentence,
   "Prospectors followed the Oregon Trail to California gold mines,"
   the word *prospectors* means _____.

   A. people
   B. people running away from the law
   C. people searching for valuable minerals
   D. people wanting to move

5. Why do you think Kansas is called the "Breadbasket of America?"

   _____

   _____

   _____

   _____

   _____

   _____

KANSAS

State Facts

Nickname: _____

Became a State: _____

State Bird: _____

State Flower: _____

State Tree: _____

Fun Fact: _____

If you visit Mammoth Cave in central Kentucky, don't forget your compass and flashlight! Underground passages connect Mammoth Cave to the world's longest cave system. If all the explored passages of this system were placed end to end, you would be able to walk across the entire state without ever seeing the sky. However, you'd miss out on a lot of beautiful scenery!

Kentucky borders seven other states. With our modern highways, getting to Kentucky from any of these states is as easy as getting into your car. Yet it wasn't always so simple. The Appalachian Mountains in eastern Kentucky were a natural barrier for white settlers crossing from the eastern colonies. American pioneers such as Daniel Boone searched for a path through the mountains. Eventually, they found the Cumberland Gap. This was the crossing point from Tennessee and Virginia into Kentucky. The Cumberland Gap was a deep, narrow pass, not even wide enough for a wagon. So, settlers had to walk. Between 1775 and 1800, more than 200,000 people passed through this narrow gap.

Beyond Cumberland Gap, settlers found land with everything they needed: fertile soil for growing tobacco, mountain forests filled with timber, and blue-green pastures to feed cattle and horses—especially race horses. The bluegrass area around Lexington and Frankfort, the state capital, produces some of the world's fastest thoroughbred horses. The Kentucky Derby is a famous horse race. It has been held in Louisville every year since 1875.

The Cumberland Gap didn't remain the only passage into Kentucky. Steamboats soon chugged up and down the Mississippi and Ohio Rivers, carrying crops out of the state. Trains click-clacked across the land. Huge supplies of coal and *hydroelectric power* (power generated by water) welcomed industry. Kentucky is still a leader in tobacco and coal production. Manufacturing (machinery, electronics, and food processing) employs many people, too.

When you finish investigating Mammoth Cave's underground passages, head for the Cumberland Gap. You can still walk part of Daniel Boone's original Wilderness Road across the rugged Cumberland Mountains. But you don't have to. Now you can drive. A modern tunnel runs right through the mountain.

Colorful Kentucky

Kentucky is anything but dull, but what would you expect from a state with the nickname "Bluegrass State?" Colors of all shades can be seen throughout Kentucky.

Below is a list of phrases related to the "Bluegrass State." All the missing words are color words. Use an atlas or encyclopedia to fill in the missing words.

1. A large city in southwestern Kentucky

    Bowling ___ ___ ___ ___ ___

2. Kentucky's highest mountain; located on the Kentucky-Virginia border

    ___ ___ ___ ___ ___ Mountain

3. Major tributary of the Ohio River; runs through Mammoth Cave National Park

    ___ ___ ___ ___ ___ River

4. Site of the last battle of the American Revolution (1782); located northeast of Lexington

    ___ ___ ___ ___ Licks Battlefield State Park

5. Battle between Kentucky tobacco farmers and tobacco companies between 1904-1909

    ___ ___ ___ ___ ___ Patch War

6. Type of woodpecker found in Kentucky

    ___ ___ ___ ___ ___ ___ - bellied Sapsucker

7. Winner of the 1907 Kentucky Derby

    ___ ___ ___ ___ Star

8. Another name for the tulip tree, Kentucky's state tree

    ___ ___ ___ ___ ___ ___ Poplar

9. A type of sunfish (or panfish) commonly found in Kentucky's lakes and rivers

    ___ ___ ___ ___ gill

Comprehension Questions

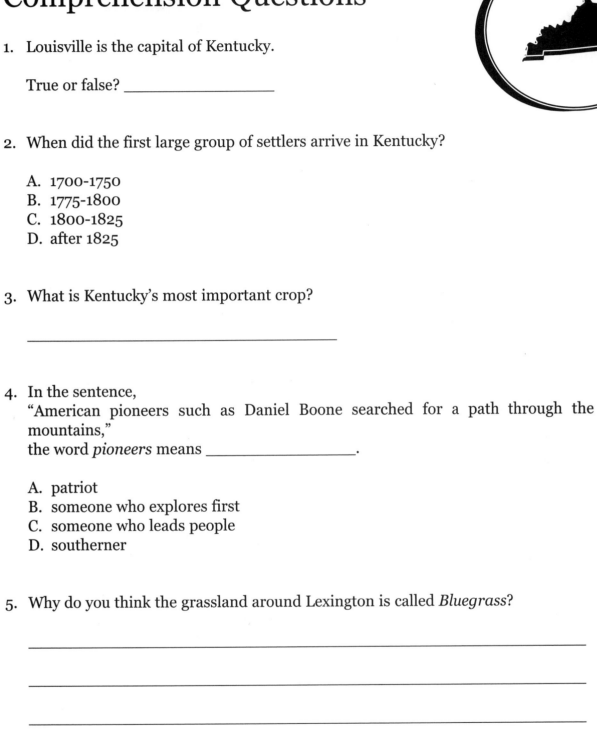

1. Louisville is the capital of Kentucky.

   True or false? _____

2. When did the first large group of settlers arrive in Kentucky?

   A. 1700-1750
   B. 1775-1800
   C. 1800-1825
   D. after 1825

3. What is Kentucky's most important crop?

   _____

4. In the sentence,
   "American pioneers such as Daniel Boone searched for a path through the mountains,"
   the word *pioneers* means _____.

   A. patriot
   B. someone who explores first
   C. someone who leads people
   D. southerner

5. Why do you think the grassland around Lexington is called *Bluegrass*?

   _____

   _____

   _____

   _____

   _____

State Facts

Nickname: _____

Became a State: _____

State Bird: _____

State Flower: _____

State Tree: _____

Fun Fact: _____

No other state is easier to recognize than Louisiana. It looks like a boot stepping into the Gulf of Mexico—splat! If this is your boot, be prepared to get wet feet. The hole at your toe is Lake Pontchartrain, a *brackish* (partly saltwater) lake north of New Orleans. Everywhere you step you'll find rivers and marshes. Not all the water comes from below. Louisiana is one of the country's rainiest states.

The Mississippi River pours into the Gulf of Mexico at New Orleans, Louisiana's largest city. This ocean port was the European gateway to America. Louisiana was a colony of France, Spain, then France again before it was bought by the United States in 1803. The Louisiana Purchase cost about $15,000,000, and included extra land that became all or part of 13 states. What a deal!

Evidence of French and Spanish settlement can still be heard in southern Louisiana where many people speak French. The Creoles are descendants of early French and Spanish settlers. The Cajuns are descendants of 18th-century French-Canadians. Also, one-third of Louisiana's population is African-American. We can thank Louisiana's rich, varied heritage for New Orleans' annual Mardi Gras celebration, for spicy Cajun food, and for being the "Birthplace of Jazz."

Most of Louisiana was once part of an ancient bay of the Gulf of Mexico. Eventually, *silt* (soil carried by moving water) built up the land around this bay, forming Louisiana. Many of Louisiana's rivers rise higher than the surrounding land. The risk of flooding is great. Louisianans have built levees to form barriers along river banks. Natural *bayous* (swampy river outlets) catch river overflow. The soil here is extremely fertile. Cotton and sugarcane are still grown. But oil and natural gas are more important. The manufacturing of chemicals and transportation equipment is big in cities such as Shreveport, Baton Rouge (the capital), and Lake Charles.

Despite the swamps, trees cover half the state. Louisiana has a huge variety of plant and animal life. Your boots will protect your toes from crawfish, but watch out for the alligators!

Which One of These Things Is Not Like the Others?

Listed below are 11 sets of Louisiana facts. Each fact is identified with a letter. Only three facts are correct in each group. Use an encyclopedia, atlas, or another resource to determine which facts are incorrect. Circle the incorrect facts.

1. Major Louisiana cities

   G. Lafayette
   H. New Orleans
   I. Shreveport
   J. Vicksburg

2. States larger than Louisiana

   C. Arizona
   D. Georgia
   E. Tennessee
   F. Utah

3. Famous Louisianan jazz musicians

   A. Dizzy Gillespie
   B. Fats Domino
   C. Jelly Roll Morton
   D. Louis Armstrong

4. Early Spanish explorers in Louisiana

   K. Alonso Álvarez de Pineda (1519)
   L. Alvar Núñez Cabeza de Vaca (1528)
   M. Hernando de Soto (1541)
   N. René Robert Cavelier, Sieur de La Salle (1682)

5. States with fewer people than Louisiana

   J. Idaho
   K. Nevada
   L. North Carolina
   M. Utah

6. States that border Louisiana

   A. Alabama
   B. Arkansas
   C. Mississippi
   D. Texas

7. States created from the Louisiana Purchase

   F. California
   G. Louisiana
   H. Missouri
   I. Oklahoma

8. Major Louisiana lakes

   C. Calcasieu Lake
   D. Catahoula Lake
   E. Lake Pontchartrain
   F. Wright Patman Lake

9. Major Louisiana rivers

   H. Atchafalaya River
   I. Missouri River
   J. Sabine River
   K. Tensas River

10. Symbols on the 2002 Louisiana Commemorative Quarter

   T. cypress tree
   U. horn
   V. musical notes
   W. pelican

11. Words in the state motto

   C. Confidence
   D. Justice
   E. Liberty
   F. Union

Who was the famous Louisianan pirate who helped defeat the British in the 1815 Battle of New Orleans? To find out, write the letters of the incorrect facts in the blanks below, in the order it is listed under each blank.

Fact #   1   2   3   4   5   6   7   8   9   10   11

Comprehension Questions

1. Louisiana is very wet.

   True or false? _____

2. From which country did the United States buy Louisiana?

   A. Britain
   B. France
   C. Mexico
   D. Spain

3. What are descendants of French-Canadians in Louisiana called?

   _____

4. In the sentence,
   "Louisiana has a huge variety of plant and animal life,"
   the word *variety* means _____.

   A. number of different kinds
   B. picture
   C. selection of wet things
   D. strange

5. Look at a map. The state of Louisiana is shaped like a boot. What river might represent the laces of that boot? Why?

   _____

   _____

   _____

   _____

   _____

LOUISIANA

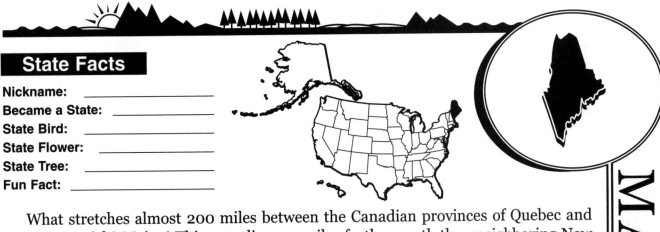

State Facts

Nickname: _____
Became a State: _____
State Bird: _____
State Flower: _____
State Tree: _____
Fun Fact: _____

What stretches almost 200 miles between the Canadian provinces of Quebec and New Brunswick? Maine! This state lies 150 miles further north than neighboring New Hampshire. It is the largest New England state. And if you are camped out on West Quoddy Head peninsula in eastern Maine, you are as far east as the country gets.

The state's population is concentrated in southern Maine. Most of the original settlers came from Massachusetts. Maine remained part of Massachusetts until 1820, when it became the 23rd state. Even then, the Canadian borders weren't clear. It nearly took a war between the British (who held the Canadian lands) and the Mainers to settle that argument. This was the first of many peaceful agreements between Canada and the United States. Many Mainers proudly claim French-Canadians as their ancestors.

All of Maine's major cities lie in the south. Portland, the largest, is an important trading port on the Atlantic Ocean. The capital city, Augusta, was built on the Kennebec River. Maine's southern coast is covered in sandy beaches and salt marshes. The further northeast you go, the rockier and more uneven the coast becomes. Mount Desert Island is the most spectacular of Maine's many islands. It is crowned with Cadillac Mountain. This is the nation's highest point on the Atlantic coast.

Lumbering has always been important in the "Pine Tree State." Shipbuilding was Maine's first industry. Today, paper and wood products are still manufactured. Fishing is significant, especially for lobster. But, don't let all the rocks and forests fool you. Maine is one of the country's leaders in growing potatoes!

Northern Maine's wilderness remains untouched. Camping is the best way to visit the thousands of lakes beyond the Longfellow Mountains. Roads here are few, if any! While you're munching on blueberries, watch out for black bears. And, shh . . . look up, way up—did you see that moose?

Down East in Maine

Use an atlas, encyclopedia, or another resource to help you complete the crossword puzzle.

Across

4. Maine is close to this ocean.
7. Maine became a slave-free state in 1820. This was part of the 1820 _ _ _ _ _ _ _ _ Compromise.
8. Most of Maine's potatoes are grown in the _ _ _ _ _ _ _ _ _ Plateau.
9. This largest member of the deer family is a common sight in northern Maine.
11. The city of Bangor is on the Penobscot _ _ _ _ _.
12. Maine's tallest mountain.
14. Maine's state tree.
15. Author Harriet Beecher _ _ _ _ _ _ was most famous for her anti-slavery novel, "Uncle Tom's Cabin." She wrote this book while living in Brunswick, Maine.
16. Maine's tallest mountain is in Baxter State _ _ _ _.

Down

1. Poland Spring is a resort town north of Portland. The spring here is the source for bottled Poland Spring _ _ _ _ _.
2. ME is the postal abbreviation for _ _ _ _ _.
3. The St. _ _ _ _ _ River flows into Passamaquoddy Bay at Calais, Maine.
5. This crustacean is Maine's most important catch.
6. Portland is on this ocean bay.
7. Maine is one of the eight states that begin with the letter M. Its postal abbreviation is _ _.
10. _ _ _ Orchard Beach in southern Maine has one of the longest sand beaches on the east coast.
12. Maine's state bird.
13. Ogunquit is a popular summer resort for artists (and people who love _ _ _).

Use the first letters of your clue answers to find out the name of the largest lake in Maine.

___ ___ ___ ___ E H E ___ D ___ ___ K E
7A 10D 10D 15A   4A   5D 4A

Comprehension Questions

1. Maine stretches further east than Massachusetts.

   True or false? _____

2. Which of the following geographic landmarks is NOT found in Maine?

   A. Cadillac Mountain
   B. Cape Cod
   C. Mount Desert Island
   D. West Quoddy Head

3. Name the two Canadian provinces that border Maine.

   _____

   _____

4. In the sentence,
   "The state's population is concentrated in southern Maine,"
   the word *concentrated* means _____.

   A. centered
   B. people
   C. studied
   D. thin

5. Maine's tall, straight pine trees were very important to early shipbuilders. In those days, sailing ships were made of wood. What part of the ship do you think these trees were used for? Why?

   _____

   _____

   _____

   _____

MARYLAND

State Facts

Nickname: _____
Became a State: _____
State Bird: _____
State Flower: _____
State Tree: _____
Fun Fact: _____

Baltimore is the largest city in Maryland. Almost half of the state's population lives in or close to this city. Maryland's state bird is the orange-and-black Baltimore Oriole. The name Baltimore came from Lord Baltimore of Britain. Orange and black are the colors of Lord Baltimore's family crest. Even the Maryland state capital, Annapolis, was named for a family member, because Lady Baltimore's name was Anne. In 1632, King Charles I of England gave Lord Baltimore permission to start a colony in the Chesapeake Bay area. Baltimore did, and Maryland was born.

Maryland is an oddly shaped state. The Chesapeake Bay splits the state into two uneven pieces. The small Eastern Shore shares the Delmarva Peninsula with Delaware and Virginia. The larger Western Shore is made up of land between the Potomac River and Chesapeake Bay. What about the rectangular bite out of southern Maryland? That land was donated to make room for Washington, D.C., the nation's capital. The only Maryland border that is easy to draw is the northern border. This border is part of the Mason-Dixon Line. Before the Civil War, this line separated the states that allowed slavery from the states that didn't. Maryland was a slave state. Luckily for Washington, D.C., Maryland remained within the Union during the Civil War.

Chesapeake Bay teems with blue crabs, just as it did thousands of years ago. The Allegheny Mountains in western Maryland are still thickly forested. But, some things have changed. In Lord Baltimore's time, most colonists grew tobacco. Today, farmers raise broiler chickens and dairy cattle. Maryland's *proximity* (closeness) to the federal capital has attracted government services. The state's rivers and ocean ports continue to attract trade. Maryland's population grew rapidly in the 20th century. People from poorer southern and western states came to Maryland in search of work. Many people in the Baltimore and D.C. regions work in the manufacturing of chemicals, processed foods, and other industries.

Maryland's Water Wonderland

Finding salt- or freshwater is easy in Maryland. The names of some of Maryland's waterways are listed in the word bank below. Find and circle each of these words in the puzzle, but do not find the repeated words in parentheses. (Hint: names with more than one word will be found as separate words. For example, Great and Falls in the name *Great Falls* will be found separately in the puzzle.)

Word Bank

Atlantic Ocean
Black Creek
Chesapeake and
    Delaware Canal
Chincoteague Bay
Marshyhope (Creek)
Sassafras River
Deep (Creek) Lake
Spa (Creek)
Elk (River)
Nanticoke (River)
Susquehanna (River)
Great Falls
Patuxent (River)
Tangier Sound
Gunpowder (Falls)
Pocomoke Swamp
Tar (Bay)
Hooper Strait
Port Tobacco (River)
West (River)
Liberty Reservoir
Potomac (River)
Youghiogheny (River)

Maryland's Water Wonderland

```
S A D Q V G A U P B A Y T J O C X A T C
C W T A R I V E U E W R A C A E N I M H
B R A M M F Y L A R O D C M R N A J A E
L L U M G B F K S P N A O A A R Z V R S
H I A R P S N T O U B T W H T W J P S A
T O B C I V A F O O O A E S R E M Z H P
A S O E K V E S T P L U Y Z A S X D Y E
C L U P R B E F H E Q N S I N T S R H A
S P A C E T E R D S E W U X C I A G O K
A B T Y H R Y E U H F V Q C L S S U P E
N L U P N I K S G C C U J T T A S N E L
J Q E A S O N O R T R H Z K L V A P Z V
D E E L M L I C A P A E W Y K U F O T D
D C L O A H W X O T A N E O O G R W B Z
O A C N G L H X H T L T G K X Y A D T O
F O A U M B T W O S E A U I G F S E G V
P C O R V F K K G E W A N X E R L R Z L
X Y U Q V X T E N C H V G T E R E A M D
R E S E R V O I R G V Z J U I N X A K F
N A N T I C O K E X K K T D E C T T T E
```

"Chesapeake" is a Native American word for "great shellfish bay." Chesapeake Bay is a paradise for many animals, such as clams, oysters and crabs. The Blue Crab is one of Maryland's state symbols. What kind of animal is the Blue Crab? In the top ten horizontal rows, starting with the second row, circle the first unused letter. These letters, in order, will spell the group of animals to which the blue crab belongs:

___ ___ ___ ___ ___ ___ ___ ___ ___ ___

Comprehension Questions

1. Maryland was once a colony of France.

    True or false? _____

2. Which city is the capital of Maryland?

    A. Annapolis
    B. Baltimore
    C. Chesapeake
    D. Washington

3. The Chesapeake Bay splits Maryland into two regions. Name these regions.

    _____

    _____

4. In the sentence,
    "That land was donated to make room for Washington, D.C., the nation's capital,"
    the word *donated* means _____.

    A. emptied
    B. given freely
    C. moved over
    D. sold

5. The states south of the Mason-Dixon Line were slave states. Most of these states *seceded* (withdrew) from the Union to join the Confederate States of America during the Civil War. Maryland was a slave state. Unlike its neighbor, Virginia, Maryland stayed loyal to the Union and did not join the Confederate States. The federal capital, Washington, D.C., is in the middle of Virginia and Maryland. Why was Maryland's loyalty to the Union so important?

    _____

    _____

    _____

MARYLAND

State Facts

Nickname: _____

Became a State: _____

State Bird: _____

State Flower: _____

State Tree: _____

Fun Fact: _____

MASSACHUSETTS

You don't have to be big to make a difference. Take Massachusetts, for example. This sixth smallest state was the starting point of the Revolutionary War. Without Massachusetts, there might not be an independent United States of America.

The Pilgrims landed on the shores of Cape Cod in 1620. One year later, America's first Thanksgiving was celebrated. Native Americans helped the settlers adjust to their unfamiliar new world. Within 20 years, over 12,000 English settlers had joined the Pilgrims. They formed Massachusetts Bay Colony (now the capital city, Boston) and Plymouth Colony. It was Boston, America's "Cradle of Liberty," that was the center of revolutionary activity in the late 1700s.

The "Bay State" (referring to Massachusetts Bay) is at the heart of the New England states. It is larger than Connecticut and Rhode Island to the south, but smaller than Vermont, New Hampshire, and Maine to the north. Massachusetts is dwarfed by the much-larger state of New York, its Mid-Atlantic neighbor to the west.

The rocky hill country in western Massachusetts is part of the Berkshire Hills of the Appalachian Mountains. The Connecticut River runs south through the state. The soil in the river valley is rich and fertile. The eastern lowlands of Massachusetts lie close to the Atlantic coast. Here, ponds and cranberry bogs dot the landscape. Cape Cod is shaped like a curved hook, extending eastward into the Atlantic Ocean.

With so much shoreline, no wonder shipping and whaling have played such an important part in the state's early growth. Fishing remains a major industry. The early settlers also believed in education. Boston is home to several famous medical and educational institutions.

The Commonwealth of Massachusetts is geographically small. On the contrary, the role Massachusetts played in the history of America is huge.

Lighthouse Getaway

In 1795, a group of thieves robbed a newly opened bank on one of the islands in the Cape Cod island area of Massachusetts. The thieves escaped to the mainland by stealing a lifeboat from a nearby lighthouse. Although several people were arrested for the crime, the real culprits probably went free. This event split the islanders into two groups: those who thought the real thieves had been caught, and those who didn't. Even today, no one is really sure who robbed the bank. The gold and silver coins were never recovered.

The getaway 'vehicle' came from one of the lighthouses listed below . . . but which one? To find out, plot the lighthouses from this table onto the following map. Then, decode your trail of lighthouses!

Plotting the Lighthouses

The map is drawn as a graph or grid. The line at the bottom of the graph is called the x-axis. On this map, the x-axis runs across the page from 0 to 20. The line along the left edge of the graph is called the y-axis. On this map, the y-axis runs up the page from 0 to 23.

At the top of the map is a compass rose. The x-axis at the bottom of the graph represents the west-to-east direction. The y-axis along the left of the graph represents the south-to-north direction.

Each point on the graph is identified as an ordered pair (x,y). The first number points to the x-axis. The second number points to the y-axis.

Every lighthouse has its own ordered pair and its own decoding letter. For example, the Brant Point Lighthouse has an ordered pair of (16,3) and a decoding letter of **R**.

To plot this lighthouse on the map, start with the x-axis (west-to-east). Count 16 spaces across the x-axis. Then, from that point count 3 more spaces up the y-axis. This one has been done for you, so there is already an **R** at this position.

Lighthouse and Location	(x, y)
Brant Point Light	(16,3)
Cape **P**oge Lighthouse	(8,5)
Cha**t**ham Lighthouse	(18,12)
East Ch**o**p Lighthouse	(6,6)
Edgar**t**own Lighthouse	(7,4)
G**a**y Head Light	(1,3)
Great Point Lighthouse	(17,4)
Highland Lighthouse	(16,21)
Hyannis Harbor Light	(11,12)
Junip**e**r Point Light	(3,8)
Lon**g** Point Lighthouse	(14,21)
Nauset Beach Lighthouse	(19,16)
Nobska Point Lighth**ou**se	(5,8)
Race Poin**t** Lighthouse	(12,22)
Sandy Neck Lighth**o**use	(10,13)
Sankaty H**e**ad Lighthouse	(18,2)
Stage Harbor **L**ight	(17,12)
West Chop **L**ighthouse	(5,7)
Wing**s** Neck Light	(4,11)
Wood End Lig**h**thouse	(13,21)

Plot the other lighthouses on the map, labeling them with the decoding letters from the table.

Decoding the Lighthouse Trail

Use the decoding letters that you have drawn on the map to fill in the following blanks. The clues name an island.

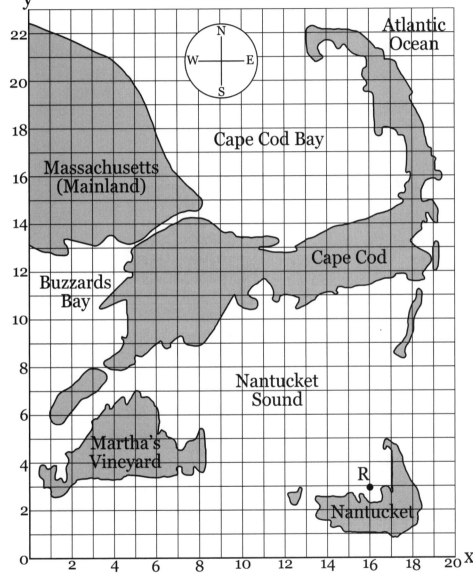

Clue 1: Nantucket's code letters, in order from north to south.

——
——
——

Clue 2: Martha's Vineyard's code letters, in order from south to north.

——
——
——

Clue 3: Cape Cod's code letters, in order from east to west

——
——
——
——
——
——
——
——

Which lighthouse lost its lifeboat on the night of the robbery?

_____

Which island was robbed? _____

Comprehension Questions

1. Massachusetts is larger than Connecticut.

   True or false? _____

2. Which of the following is NOT considered a New England State?

   A. Connecticut
   B. New Hampshire
   C. New York
   D. Vermont

3. On which shore of Massachusetts did the Pilgrims first land?

   _____

4. In the sentence,
   "Native Americans helped the settlers adjust to their unfamiliar new world,"
   the word *adjust* means _____.

   A. change
   B. discover
   C. fight
   D. understand

5. Why do you think shipbuilding is not as important an industry today as it was in the past?

   _____

   _____

   _____

   _____

   _____

   _____

MASSACHUSETTS

State Facts

Nickname: _____

Became a State: _____

State Bird: _____

State Flower: _____

State Tree: _____

Fun Fact: _____

MICHIGAN

Traveling between Michigan's Lower and Upper Peninsulas used to be difficult, especially if you were scared of water. The Straits of Mackinac join Lake Michigan and Lake Superior, but they also split Michigan into two pieces. Until 1957, people wanting to travel between the peninsulas had two choices: take a boat across the five-mile wide Straits of Mackinac, or drive 850 miles around Lake Michigan, passing through Indiana, Illinois, and Wisconsin on the way. Thanks to the "Big Mac" Bridge, today even the most fearful can drive across the Straits in just ten minutes!

There's plenty of water in Michigan to fear—and to enjoy. In the Chippewa language, the word *Michigan* means "Great Water." This state borders four of the five Great Lakes. Rivers and canals connect these lakes to each other, forming the western end of the St. Lawrence Great Lakes Waterway. Ships load up in Michigan's ports and head east to the Atlantic Ocean. Even inland, you are not far from water. Thousands of smaller lakes are sprinkled throughout the state. Swimmers, boaters, and fishing enthusiasts have plenty to do in Michigan. You don't have to get your feet wet in Michigan, but you'll have more fun if you do!

Michigan started out as a land of trappers and traders. Copper mining and lumbering in the Upper Peninsula brought settlers into the region. Iron ore is still mined in the forested Upper Peninsula. The Lower Peninsula is a source of natural gas and petroleum. Farmland covers much of southern Michigan. The fertile land along Lake Michigan's shores produces apples, cherries, and other fruit. But what really "drives" Michigan today is the automobile industry. The Detroit area, also knows as "Motor City," is home to the three largest car companies in the country.

Most people live in Michigan's Lower Peninsula. Lansing, the capital, is only one of many large cities in the region. The Upper Peninsula is smaller both in size and population. This northern region has something that its southern partner does not—Lake Superior, the largest freshwater lake in the world.

Crossing the Straits of Mackinac

MICHIGAN

The water that separates the rabbit-shaped Upper Peninsula from the mitten-shaped Lower Peninsula of Michigan is called the "Straits of Mackinac."

Listed below are the names of various places found in Michigan. Fill in the blanks with L (Lower Peninsula) or U (Upper Peninsula), according to where they are on a map. Use an atlas or encyclopedia to help you.

____ **A**nn Arbor
____ **K**eweenaw Peninsula
____ Macki**n**aw City
____ **D**etroit
____ **E**scanaba
____ Grand Ra**p**ids
____ Kalamaz**o**o
____ Pictured Rocks National **L**akeshore
____ Sau**l**t Ste. Marie
____ **P**orcupine Mountains
____ **S**aginaw Bay
____ Ba**tt**le Creek
____ Lake **G**ogebic
____ St. **Ig**nace

Question: Why is Battle Creek, Michigan known as the "Cereal Bowl of America?"
Answer: This city produces more breakfast cereal than any other place in the country. The first flaked cereal was created in Battle Creek over 100 years ago.

Using the answers above, fill in the following blanks to discover the names of the two men who started this tasty industry.

Upper Peninsula **bold** letters (in order)

____ ____ ____ ____ ____ ____

Lower Peninsula **bold** letters (in order)

____ ____ ____   ____ ____ ____ ____

Comprehension Questions

1. In Michigan, the Upper Peninsula lies south of the Lower Peninsula.

   True or false? _____

2. Which is the largest of the following Great Lakes?

   A. Lake Erie
   B. Lake Huron
   C. Lake Michigan
   D. Lake Superior

3. What mineral is mined in the Upper Peninsula?

   _____

4. In the sentence,
   "Swimmers, boaters, and fishing enthusiasts have plenty to do in Michigan,"
   the word *enthusiasts* means _____.

   A. people who enjoy doing something
   B. people who fish
   C. people who hunt
   D. people who try doing something

5. Michigan is sometimes called the "Wolverine State." A wolverine is a ferocious, thick-furred mammal found in the northern United States. How do you think Michigan got this nickname?

   _____

   _____

   _____

   _____

   _____

MICHIGAN

MINNESOTA

State Facts

Nickname: _____

Became a State: _____

State Bird: _____

State Flower: _____

State Tree: _____

Fun Fact: _____

If you've never heard the cry of a loon, come to the "North Star State." The common loon is Minnesota's state bird. In summer, the northern lakes echo with the loon's laughing call. It's a sound you won't forget.

Lakes aren't in short supply in this Midwestern state. They are everywhere, particularly in northeastern Minnesota. The rock in this area is so hard that even glaciers had a tough time wearing it away. This is part of the Canadian Shield—the land here is rocky and the lakes are deep. The biggest lake of them all is Lake Superior. Along with these thousands of lakes are rivers: the Mississippi, the Red, and countless more. In summer, this water provides swimming, boating, and fishing for Minnesotans and tourists alike. In winter, people rev up their snowmobiles and head for ice-fishing holes.

Minnesota isn't just a water wonderland. It's also one of the country's top agricultural states. Farmland covers southern Minnesota. Dairy farms produce milk. Farmers raise hogs and beef cattle. Fertile soil produces corn, soybeans, and wheat.

Although French fur traders explored Minnesota in the 17th century, Minnesota didn't become a state until 1857. By then, the Dakota, Sioux, and Ojibwe (Chippewa) Indians had signed treaties giving up their land west of the Mississippi River. Farming, lumbering, and mining enticed Americans westward. Northern European immigrants followed. Many farming communities today remain distinctly European, but several Sioux and Ojibwe Indian Reservations are also located in Minnesota.

A small lake in central Minnesota marks the start of the Mississippi River's 2,300-mile journey to the Gulf of Mexico. One of the first busy areas that the Mississippi River runs through is the Minneapolis-St. Paul area, Minnesota's "Twin Cities." Almost half of all Minnesotans live in or near these two cities. St. Paul is the state capital. Minneapolis is a major financial center. Along with nearby Rochester, these cities manufacture food products, computers, and books. Duluth, on Lake Superior, is a shipping port for grain and iron ore.

Getting Wet in Minnesota

Rivers and lakes are a common sight in Minnesota. Listed below are the names of 16 bodies of water found in Minnesota. Each river or lake is labeled on the map with a letter. With the help of an atlas or encyclopedia, write the matching letter next to each body of water on the list.

MINNESOTA

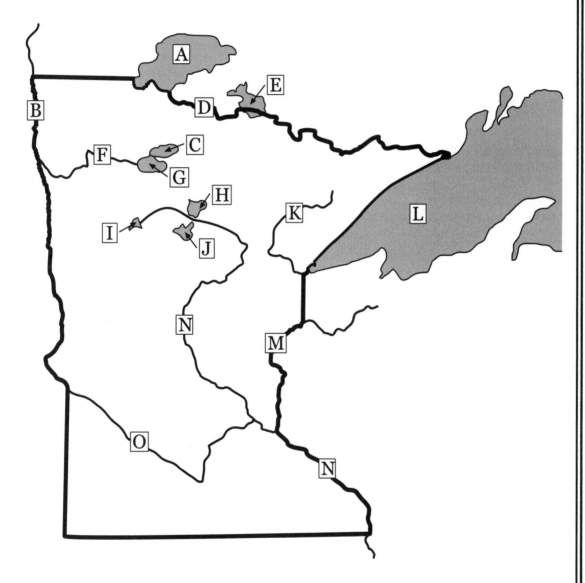

_____Lake Itasca
(the start of the
Mississippi River)

_____Lake of the Woods

_____Lake Superior

_____Lake Winnibigoshish

_____Leech Lake

_____Lower Red Lake

_____Minnesota River

_____Mississippi River

_____Rainy Lake

_____Rainy River

_____Red Lake River

_____Red River

_____St. Croix River

_____St. Louis River

_____Upper Red Lake

MINNESOTA

Comprehension Questions

1. Southern Minnesota is part of the rocky Canadian Shield.

   True or false? _____

2. Which of the following cities is located on a large lake?

   A. Duluth
   B. Minneapolis
   C. Rochester
   D. St. Paul

3. Name two important rivers that run through Minnesota or along Minnesota's borders.

   _____

   _____

4. In the sentence,
   "Farming, lumbering, and mining enticed Americans westward,"
   the word *enticed* means _____.

   A. attracted by offering hope of reward
   B. forced by hunger
   C. made them go
   D. worked

5. The Minnesota River meets the mighty Mississippi River at Minneapolis. The name Minneapolis comes from two separate words: "minne," an American-Indian word; and "polis," a Greek word for "city." Can you think of some possible meanings for the word "minne?" Why did you choose these meanings?

   _____

   _____

   _____

State Facts

Nickname: _____

Became a State: _____

State Bird: _____

State Flower: _____

State Tree: _____

Fun Fact: _____

Remember Alabama, the state shaped like your left foot? Well, put your right foot down, and that's Mississippi. Your big toe is soaking in the warm waters of the Mississippi Sound. This is the strip of water between the Mississippi coast and several offshore islands in the Gulf of Mexico. Your toe will be just one of many other toes in the Biloxi area because hundreds of tourists visit Mississippi's beaches every winter in search of sun, sand, and seafood.

Before the first Spanish and French settlers arrived, Mississippi was home to thousands of Native Americans. The Natchez, Chickasaw, and Chocktaw tribes controlled most of Mississippi. Early colonists grew rice and tobacco, then cotton. West African slaves were brought to Mississippi to work on huge cotton plantations. Expanding American settlement forced Mississippi's Native Americans westward to Oklahoma, leaving Mississippi to white settlers and their slaves. By 1861, Mississippi was one of the wealthiest states in the nation. Then, the Civil War began. The "Magnolia State's" riches disappeared after Union armies destroyed Mississippi's cities, and slavery was *abolished* (forced to end). Over one-third of the state's current population is African-American—the highest percentage in the country.

Today, modern Mississippians work at furniture-making and shrimp-fishing. They manufacture clothing, transportation equipment, and electronics. They mine for *petroleum* (oil) and natural gas. They work in financial centers such as Jackson, the state capital.

The Mississippi River flows along Mississippi's fertile western border. This mighty river is the reason America's 20th state is called "Mississippi." Mississippi is an important agricultural state. Swamps have been drained, leaving half the state suitable for farming. Cotton remains the main crop, but other crops are grown, too. Farmers grow soybeans, corn, and trees! Mississippi has more tree farms than any other state. New trees are constantly being planted to replace the older trees that have been cut down. Farmers also raise chickens, cattle, and even catfish! Mississippi is number one in freshwater catfish-farming.

MISSISSIPPI

The Natchez Trace Parkway

MISSISSIPPI

In the 1800s, pioneers used the Mississippi River as a water highway. They packed goods onto flat boats and floated down the Mississippi River to New Orleans. After they had sold all their cargo, they were ready to return home. But how? The Mississippi River only flowed in one direction—south. The pioneers wanted to go north. They walked or rode back through Mississippi along a path that came to be known as the Natchez Trace. You can still walk (or drive) the Natchez Trace Parkway today.

Below is a map of Mississippi. It shows the Natchez Trace Parkway, with various towns marked along the way. The numbers on the map represent the number of miles between towns. Using the numbers, answer the questions about the Natchez Trace.

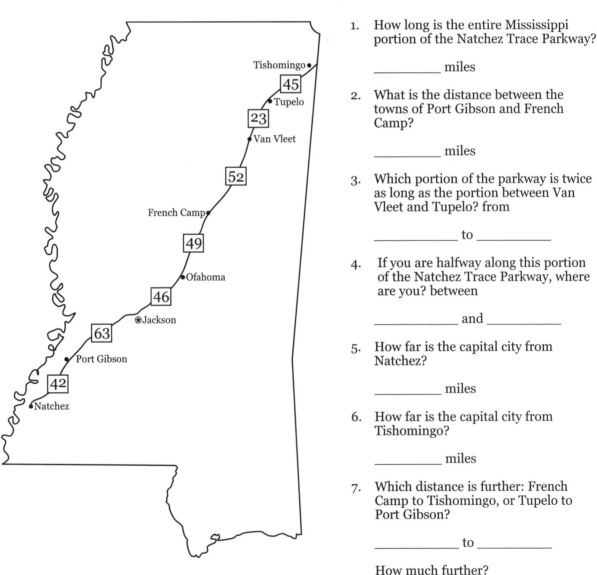

1. How long is the entire Mississippi portion of the Natchez Trace Parkway?

   _____ miles

2. What is the distance between the towns of Port Gibson and French Camp?

   _____ miles

3. Which portion of the parkway is twice as long as the portion between Van Vleet and Tupelo? from

   _____ to _____

4. If you are halfway along this portion of the Natchez Trace Parkway, where are you? between

   _____ and _____

5. How far is the capital city from Natchez?

   _____ miles

6. How far is the capital city from Tishomingo?

   _____ miles

7. Which distance is further: French Camp to Tishomingo, or Tupelo to Port Gibson?

   _____ to _____

   How much further?

   _____ miles

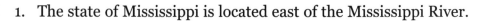

Comprehension Questions

1. The state of Mississippi is located east of the Mississippi River.

    True or false? _____

2. Which of the following Native American tribes did NOT live in the Mississippi area?

    A. Chickasaw
    B. Chocktaw
    C. Natchez
    D. Shoshone

3. What is the state capital of Mississippi?

    _____

4. In the sentence,
    "By 1861, Mississippi was one of the wealthiest states in the nation,"
    the word *wealthiest* means _____.

    A. busiest
    B. emptiest
    C. happiest
    D. richest

5. The 1863 Battle of Vicksburg was a turning point in the Civil War. Vicksburg, Mississippi lies halfway between New Orleans, Louisiana, and Memphis, Tennessee. All these cities are on the Mississippi River. The Mississippi is a major transportation route between the Gulf of Mexico and the Great Lakes. During the Civil War, Mississippi, Louisiana, and Tennessee were part of the Confederate States of America. Before the Battle of Vicksburg, Confederate (southern) troops were in control of Vicksburg. After the Battle of Vicksburg, Union (northern) troops took over the city. Why do you think this battle was so important for the eventual Union victory?

    _____

    _____

    _____

    _____

MISSISSIPPI

MISSOURI

Missouri was part of an 1803 deal between the United States and France called the Louisiana Purchase. Getting the city of St. Louis, as well as the junction of these two rivers, was one of the bonuses of that deal. In 1804, President Thomas Jefferson sent out an expedition to explore the Louisiana Purchase territory. Army officers Lewis and Clarke started their two-year journey from—you guessed it!—St. Louis, Missouri.

Missouri's cities have played major roles in America's history. Westbound pioneers on the Santa Fe and Oregon Trails stocked up on supplies in Independence, Missouri, before heading into the wilderness. The fur trade centered around the city of St. Louis, Missouri. The Pony Express, an early mail-delivery system that stretched to California, started at St. Joseph, Missouri. And Jefferson City, Missouri's capital, was a welcome stopping-point for steamboats chugging along the Missouri River.

Missouri borders eight other states. Some of these shared boundaries are less than 50 miles long—Nebraska, Oklahoma, Tennessee, and Kentucky. The other boundaries are hundreds of miles long—Iowa, Illinois, Arkansas, and Kansas. But, it's only in the "Show Me" state of Missouri that the nation's two longest rivers meet. The muddy Missouri River runs along the northwestern corner of Missouri. This river turns east at Kansas City and then flows across the state to the city of St. Louis. There it joins up with the mighty Mississippi River, ending the Missouri River's 2,500-mile run.

In the north of Missouri, above the Missouri River, are fertile plains. In the south is the hilly Ozark Plateau. Underground caves and gushing springs are common sights in the Ozarks' forested hills. Missouri has long been an important agricultural state. Farmers raise beef cattle and hogs, and grow soybeans, corn, and hay. They harvest apples, peaches, and strawberries. Manufacturing is also important to Missouri. St. Louis and Kansas City are industrial giants in the Midwest. Transportation equipment and food products are their specialties. Trucks, trains, barges, and planes loaded with goods travel in and out of these cities.

Finally, Missouri enjoys tourism as a profitable industry, in part because the Gateway Arch is a popular place to visit. In 1935, St. Louis was chosen as the site of a new monument to commemorate the expansion of the United States to the West. Completed in 1965, the nation's tallest monument provides a fitting tribute to pioneering spirit.

Crossing Waters in Missouri

MISSOURI

Use an atlas, encyclopedia, or another resource to help you complete the crossword puzzle.

Down

1. Missouri author _ _ _ _ Twain created the characters of Tom Sawyer and Huckleberry Finn.
2. Ice cream _ _ _ _ _ were first introduced at the 1904 St. Louis World's Fair.
3. Taum _ _ _ _ Mountain is the highest point in Missouri.
4. Missouri's nickname is the "Show _ _ State."
5. The 1804 _ _ _ _ _ and Clark Expedition started out from St. Louis.
6. Missouri bank robber _ _ _ _ _ James was killed by a member of his own gang.
7. In 1682, French explorer René Robert Cavelier, Sieur de la _ _ _ _ _ claimed the Missouri area for France.
8. Cotton candy was called _ _ _ _ _ floss at the 1904 St. Louis World's Fair.
10. This state is located directly south of Missouri.
14. This is Missouri's most plentiful metal.

Across

2. The city of St. _ _ _ _ _ _ _ was the first capital of Missouri (1821-1825).
6. _ _ _ _ _ _ _ _ _ City has been the capital of Missouri since 1826.
9. The _ _ _ _ _ Fe Trail started in Independence.
11. The _ _ _ Moines River joins the Mississippi River in the northeast corner of Missouri.
12. Between 1762 and 1800, the Missouri area belonged to the country of _ _ _ _ _ _.
13. Missouri pilot Charles Lindbergh was the first person to fly solo across the Atlantic. The name of his plane was "The _ _ _ _ _ of St. Louis."

Use the first letters of your clue answers to find out the name of Missouri's official state animal.

The ___ ___ ___ ___ O U R ___ ___ U ___ E
    4D 14D 9A 3D   14D   4D   5D

Comprehension Questions

1. The Missouri River runs along the entire western border of Missouri.

   True or false? _____

2. Approximately how long is the Missouri River?

   A. 1,803 miles
   B. 1,821 miles
   C. 2,000 miles
   D. 2,500 miles

3. What is Missouri's hilly region called?

   _____

4. In the sentence,
   "Getting the city of St. Louis, as well as the junction of these two rivers, was one of the bonuses of that deal,"
   the word *junction* means _____.

   A. ending point
   B. flowing
   C. place of joining
   D. riverbed

5. Why do you think the city of St. Louis was the center of the fur trade?

   _____

   _____

   _____

   _____

   _____

MISSOURI

State Facts

Nickname: _____
Became a State: _____
State Bird: _____
State Flower: _____
State Tree: _____
Fun Fact: _____

MONTANA

Take your pick: big open sky of the Great Plains, or icy glaciers of the majestic Rocky Mountains? Stretching over 600 miles east-to-west along the Canadian border, Montana has both. The Continental Divide cuts through Montana's mountains, while the plains take up the eastern three-fifths of the state. All rivers east of this imaginary line drain into the Gulf of Mexico or Hudson Bay. All rivers west of the divide empty into the Pacific Ocean.

Eastern Montana's rolling prairie used to be home to millions of buffalo. This grassland was purchased from France in 1803. Western Montana's mountains are rich in silver and gold. These peaks became part of the United States after the signing of the 1846 Oregon Treaty with Great Britain. Montana became a state in 1889.

Before the 1805 Lewis and Clark expedition, Montana's Native Americans lived with little European interference. The Blackfeet, Atsina, Kootenai, Shoshone, and Crow tribes all shared Montana's vast lands. The success of President Thomas Jefferson's expedition changed all that. When gold was discovered in 1862, eager prospectors rushed in to make their fortunes. On the prairie, wild buffalo were killed and replaced by domestic cattle. The Battles of Little Bighorn and Big Hole Prairie in the 1870s were the nation's last major Native American battles. The expansion of the railroad brought more settlers. Native Americans were forced onto reservations. Cowboys and ranching became a way of life.

Montana is one of the least densely populated states in the country. There is plenty of space to roam in this "Treasure State." Perhaps this is why Montana's natural resources remain so abundant—endless grassland for cattle, fertile soil for wheat, deep reserves of coal and oil, rich deposits of metals, and acres upon acres of trees. Even now, visitors still enjoy the same big sky as settlers did so long ago.

Montana's Mountains

The Rocky Mountains run through western Montana. They are made up of many smaller mountain ranges, such as the Beartooth, Absaroka, and Bitterroot Mountains. Some of the highest peaks in these mountain ranges are shown in the graph below. Use this chart to answer the following questions about these Montana mountains.

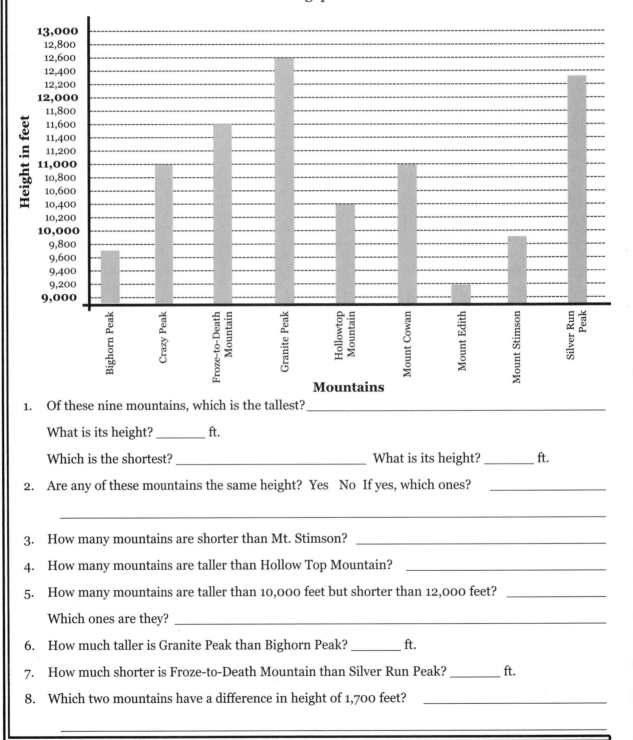

1. Of these nine mountains, which is the tallest? _____

   What is its height? _____ ft.

   Which is the shortest? _____ What is its height? _____ ft.

2. Are any of these mountains the same height? Yes   No   If yes, which ones? _____

   _____

3. How many mountains are shorter than Mt. Stimson? _____

4. How many mountains are taller than Hollow Top Mountain? _____

5. How many mountains are taller than 10,000 feet but shorter than 12,000 feet? _____

   Which ones are they? _____

6. How much taller is Granite Peak than Bighorn Peak? _____ ft.

7. How much shorter is Froze-to-Death Mountain than Silver Run Peak? _____ ft.

8. Which two mountains have a difference in height of 1,700 feet? _____

   _____

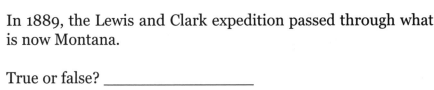

Comprehension Questions

MONTANA

1. In 1889, the Lewis and Clark expedition passed through what is now Montana.

   True or false? _____

2. Which of the following is NOT an important resource in Montana?

   A. coal
   B. fish
   C. lumber
   D. wheat

3. The Oregon Treaty was an agreement between what two countries?

   _____

   _____

4. In the phrase,
   "Perhaps this is why Montana's natural resources remain so abundant," the word *abundant* means _____.

   A. beautiful
   B. clean
   C. plentiful
   D. scarce

5. Two nicknames for Montana are the "Treasure State" and "Big Sky Country." Why do you think those nicknames are appropriate?

   _____

   _____

   _____

   _____

NEBRASKA

In 1820, an Army Major passed through Nebraska on an expedition to the Rocky Mountains. Unimpressed, he described the land as a desert "unfit for farming." Nebraska stretches from the Missouri River to the foothills of the Rocky Mountains. It has blossomed into the country's leading agricultural state, and the Major probably wouldn't even recognize it today.

In their rush to reach California goldfields, travelers along the Oregon and California Trails kept their eyes peeled for one thing—the Chimney Rock landmark in Nebraska's far west. For weary travelers, this huge sandstone formation marked the end of the plains and the beginning of the mountains. The Oregon Trail followed the Platte River across Nebraska. The Platte is a major east-west branch of the great Missouri River. Today, military posts that protected travelers from Indian attacks have turned into modern towns. A major highway has replaced the Oregon Trail. But the wide, shallow Platte River remains.

Nebraska was part of the 1803 Louisiana Purchase. Although it was considered Indian Country in 1834, white settlers still arrived. Thirty years later, Nebraska officially became a territory, and the Cheyenne and Sioux Indians lost their fight to keep their land. In 1867, after the Civil War, Nebraska was accepted into the Union.

Far from the ocean, Nebraska has a continental climate: hot summers and cold winters. Winter blizzards and summer droughts occur frequently. Luckily, there is an enormous supply of underground water that is used to irrigate the land. Nebraska's richest farmland is in the southeast (near the capital of Lincoln) and also along the eastern border. The land rises gradually from east to west. Most of Nebraska lies in the treeless Great Plains. Central Nebraska is covered in sand dunes and grassland. Rain runs through the sand like a sponge, and grass keeps the sand in place. These Sand Hills are perfect for grazing cattle.

The Army Major has been proved wrong. If ever a state was "fit" for farming, it's Nebraska. No other "desert" has produced as much corn and wheat, nor fed as many cattle, as Nebraska.

N...E...B...R...A...S...K...A

Learn more about the state of Nebraska. Use a dictionary, encyclopedia, or atlas to help you fill in the blanks in the sentences below. Each of the missing words starts with the corresponding letter in the name Nebraska.

N   The Kansas—N __ __ __ __ __ __ __ Act of 1854, signed by President Franklin Pierce, expanded slavery into the two new territories that it created. People who were against slavery believed that this law was wrong. The Civil War started seven years later.

E   Nebraska's state motto is "E __ __ __ __ __ __ __ before the law."

B   The city of B __ __ __ __ __ __ __ , just south of Omaha, is the oldest permanent European settlement in Nebraska. It started in the 1820s as a fur-trading post along the Missouri River. It is now home to Offutt Air Force Base (formerly Fort Crook).

R   In 1865, the Union Pacific R __ __ __ __ __ __ __ started to build tracks westward from Omaha, Nebraska. This created the first transcontinental rail system in the country. Today, Omaha is Nebraska's largest city.

A   A __ __ __ __ Day started in Nebraska in 1872, when Nebraskan Sterling Morton decided to set aside one day each year to plant trees. In Nebraska, this day officially falls on April 22nd, Morton's birthday. Not surprisingly, the country's largest planted National Forest is found in Nebraska. One of this state's nicknames is the "Tree Planter's State."

S   Nebraska pioneers built their houses of s __ __ instead of wood, since there were few trees on the plains. These practical houses were cool in the hot summer and warm in the cold winter.

K   This town in south-central Nebraska was named for Fort K __ __ __ __ __ , a military outpost located on the opposite side of the Platte River. Instead of watching for pioneers passing along the Oregon Trail, today's residents watch for sandhill cranes and endangered whooping cranes as they fly past on their annual migration.

A   Fossils of extinct rhinoceros-like creatures from 20 million years ago have been discovered in the A __ __ __ __ Fossil Beds in northwestern Nebraska, about 20 miles south of the town of Harrison.

Comprehension Questions

1. Nebraska does not have many forests.

   True or false? _____

2. What is the name of Nebraska's capital?

   A. California
   B. Lincoln
   C. Sioux
   D. Union

3. What type of climate does Nebraska have?

   _____

4. In the sentence,
   "Winter blizzards and summer droughts occur frequently,"
   the word *droughts* means _____.

   A. dry periods
   B. rains
   C. weather
   D. wet periods

5. In the Sand Hills, ranchers are careful to prevent *overgrazing* (total stripping of the grass by grazing cattle). Why do you think ranchers have to be so careful?

   _____

   _____

   _____

   _____

   _____

   _____

   _____

State Facts

Nickname: _____

Became a State: _____

State Bird: _____

State Flower: _____

State Tree: _____

Fun Fact: _____

Whether you're in Nevada to enjoy the sunshine or the nightlife, one thing's for sure—you can leave your umbrella behind! It's the driest state in the country. Rain-filled clouds move eastward from the Pacific Ocean. They float across California, heading straight for Nevada. When they hit the Sierra Nevada, the towering mountains that run along Nevada's northwestern border cause the heavy clouds to have trouble passing over these snow-covered peaks.

Most of Nevada sits high above sea level. Nevada lies west of the Rocky Mountains and east of the Sierra Nevada. Over 100 smaller mountain ranges pop up in between, separated from each other by *buttes* (single hills), *mesas* (flat mountains), and *playas* (dry lakes). With so little rain, many of Nevada's rivers run dry during the hot summer months. Only the Colorado River, in the south, reaches the sea. Irrigation and water conservation are extremely important. The Hoover Dam was built on the Colorado River to help solve the water problem. This dam created Lake Mead, one of the world's largest artificial lakes. It supplies water to Nevada, Arizona, and southern California.

Nevada's mountains provide more than just beautiful scenery. They're full of silver, too. Miners have dug for silver and gold in these mountains for years. The desert has also been a place for digging, but not for silver and gold. During the last half of the 20th century, nuclear bombs were tested underground at the Nevada Test Site in the Mojave Desert. This test site is larger than Rhode Island.

Nevada doesn't have many large cities. The capital, Carson City, is home to only 50,000 people. On the other hand, you've probably heard of Nevada's largest city—Las Vegas. A century ago, Las Vegas was just a pile of desert sand. With the legalization of gambling in 1931, Las Vegas has grown into the entertainment capital of the world. More than half of all Nevadans live in or close to Las Vegas. Las Vegas and Reno, a city in the Sierra Nevada, are the financial and manufacturing centers of the state.

NEVADA

Whose Land Is It Anyway?

The United States government owns almost four-fifths of Nevada—that's more than any other state. Many ranchers rent land from the federal government. They graze their cattle on this rented land. Several government agencies own land in Nevada, including the Forest Service, National Park Service, and the United States Air Force.

Here is a map of Nevada and a list of some of the government-owned areas in the state. The areas are labeled on the map with letters. Use an atlas, encyclopedia, or another resource to match the letters with the areas below. Write the correct letter on the line beside each name on the list. These letters spell out the name of a national forest which is scattered throughout northern and eastern Nevada.

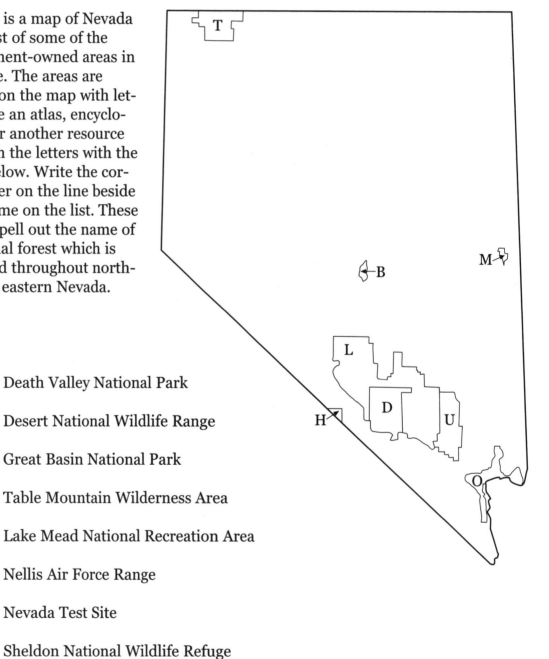

_____ Death Valley National Park

_____ Desert National Wildlife Range

_____ Great Basin National Park

_____ Table Mountain Wilderness Area

_____ Lake Mead National Recreation Area

_____ Nellis Air Force Range

_____ Nevada Test Site

_____ Sheldon National Wildlife Refuge

Comprehension Questions

1. Gambling is legal in Nevada.

   True or false? _____

2. Which of the following is NOT a city in Nevada?

   A. Carson City
   B. Hooverville
   C. Las Vegas
   D. Reno

3. What is the name of the most important river in Nevada?

   _____

4. In the sentence,
   "This dam created Lake Mead, one of the world's largest artificial lakes,"
   the word *artificial* means _____.

   A. fresh
   B. man-made
   C. natural
   D. salty

5. Why do you think the desert was chosen as a place to test nuclear bombs?

   _____

   _____

   _____

   _____

   _____

NEVADA

NEW HAMPSHIRE

State Facts

Nickname: _____
Became a State: _____
State Bird: _____
State Flower: _____
State Tree: _____
Fun Fact: _____

One New Hampshire resident has lived there for thousands of years—the Old Man of the Mountain. He lives in the Presidential Range of New Hampshire's White Mountains. When the last glaciers retreated from the side of Cannon Mountain, they left five ledges of granite rock stacked on top of each other. If you look up at these ledges, you will see the enormous profile of a stern, stone-faced man.

If you hike or ski in these mountains, you'll understand why New Hampshire is known as the "Granite State." Even glaciers had difficulty scraping away the hard granite. Occasionally the ice won the battle, leaving behind deep gashes in the rock called notches. The Old Man of the Mountain looks down at Franconia Notch, one of the most scenic spots in the state.

What if you don't like mountains? Don't worry! Windy Mount Washington might not be for you, but there are plenty of other things to do. New Hampshire's trees put on a brilliant show of leaf color in the fall. Springtime is perfect for sampling fresh maple syrup. Swimming and fishing won't be a problem. Lake Winnipesaukee is the largest of the state's many lakes, and the Connecticut River runs along the entire Vermont border. What about the ocean? New Hampshire has that, too. The "Granite State's" thirteen-mile long coastline is the shortest of any state that borders an ocean. However, these thirteen miles are packed with sandy beaches.

It's hard to believe that forested New Hampshire started as an agricultural state. There are still dairy farms, though modern New Hampshire makes more things than it grows. Electronics and machinery manufacturing are major industries in the southeastern part of the state. Manchester, the largest city, and Concord, the capital, are financial and industrial centers.

The Old Man of the Mountain hangs out with his buddies, Mounts Washington, Adams, and Jefferson, in New Hampshire's Presidential Range. Every four years, the country's first presidential primary elections are held in the Granite State. The Old Man of the Mountain is always there, keeping a watchful eye on future presidents.

Measuring Up to the
Old Man of the Mountain

In New Hampshire's White Mountain State National Forest, near Franconia Notch State Park, the Old Man of the Mountain measures about 40 feet from the bottom of his chin to the top of his forehead. How do you measure up?

Use a ruler to measure your forehead, nose, upper lip, and chin as shown in the diagram. Round these measurements to the nearest inch. Write these measurements in the blanks below, then answer the following questions about the two faces. Remember: The Old Man's measurements are in feet ('). Your measurements will be in inches ("). (Hint: There are 12 inches in 1 foot.)

F. your forehead _____"

N. your nose   _____"

L. your upper lip _____"

C. your chin   _____"

T. total length   _____"

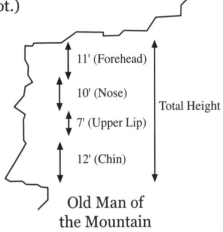

11' (Forehead)

10' (Nose)

7' (Upper Lip)

12' (Chin)

Total Height

Old Man of
the Mountain

1. What is The Old Man of the Mountain's longest facial feature (forehead, nose, upper lip, or chin)? _____
2. What is your shortest facial feature? _____
3. The Old Man of the Mountain's chin is about 12' high. What facial feature is closest to being about half the height of The Old Man of the Mountain's chin? _____
4. How long is your upper lip? _____"
    Is one or more of your facial features about twice the height of your upper lip?
    _____ (yes/no)
    If yes, which feature(s)? _____
5. How much longer is The Old Man of the Mountain's face than yours? _____
6. If you were a giant, and the measurements for your face were in feet instead of inches, would your face be longer than The Old Man of the Mountain's? _____ (yes/no)

    If yes, how much longer would your giant face be than Old Stone Face's?
    _____' How many complete Old Stone Faces, stacked on top of each other, would fit into your giant face? _____

    If no, how much longer would Old Stone Face's face be than your giant face? _____'
    How many of your complete giant faces, stacked on top of each other,
    would fit into Old Stone Face? _____

CD-0774 50 States

NEW HAMPSHIRE

Comprehension Questions

1. President Washington's nickname is the Old Man of the Mountain.

   True or false? _____

2. Which of the following are NOT names of mountains in New Hampshire?

   A. Cannon Mountain
   B. Mount Adams
   C. Mount Jefferson
   D. Mount St. Helens

3. What political event is New Hampshire famous for?

   _____

   _____

4. In the sentence,
   "If you look up at these ledges, you will see the enormous profile of a stern, stone-faced man,"
   the word *stern* means _____.

   A. large
   B. rocky
   C. smiling
   D. strict

5. How do you think the Presidential Range got its name?

   _____

   _____

   _____

   _____

   _____

State Facts

Nickname: _____

Became a State: _____

State Bird: _____

State Flower: _____

State Tree: _____

Fun Fact: _____

NEW JERSEY

Lights, camera, action! Welcome to—no, not Hollywood, but—New Jersey! In 1891, Thomas Edison invented the motion picture camera in his New Jersey laboratory. For 25 years, New Jersey was the motion picture capital of the world. Today, it's known more for its manufacturing (chemicals, food products, and printed materials) than movies. But that doesn't change history.

There's a lot more to New Jersey's history than just movies. What about George Washington's 1776 crossing of the Delaware River to capture Trenton from the British? Or the 1777 Battle of Princeton? The "Garden State" earned its nickname during the Revolutionary War for its ability to supply food to the colonies. New Jersey still uses this nickname. It's a major producer of greenhouse and plant nursery products (fruits and vegetables).

To the west of New Jersey are the Delaware River, the state of Pennsylvania, and the city of Philadelphia. To the east are the Atlantic Ocean, the Hudson River, the state of New York, and New York City. That leaves New Jersey sandwiched between two of the largest cities and the two most important rivers in the eastern United States. The New Jersey Turnpike is one of the busiest highways in the nation. It runs across the state, connecting Philadelphia with New York City.

Although New Jersey isn't big (only four states are smaller), this small slice of America is home to millions of people. Many work in neighboring Philadelphia and New York City. Most of them live in cities such as Newark, Jersey City, and Trenton, the capital. Several larger states have greater populations than New Jersey, but New Jersey is the most crowded. It has a higher population density than any other state in the country.

Southern New Jersey lies near the ocean. Not as many people live in this coastal plain, and seaside resorts outnumber factories. Each summer, thousands of vacationers visit New Jersey's beaches. A year-round attraction is Atlantic City, where gambling is legal. The annual Miss America pageant is held here. Every fall, 51 young women travel to Atlantic City, New Jersey, each one hoping to be crowned the next Miss America.

NEW JERSEY

Getting to New Jersey

If you want to travel in or out of New Jersey, you will probably cross over water. Many bridges in the state connect New Jersey cities to the neighboring states of Pennsylvania, New York, and Delaware.

Five of these bridges are listed below. Each bridge has two of the three characteristics: a New Jersey starting city, an out-of-state ending place, or the name of the water over which the bridge passes. The missing information is listed on the right side of this page. Use a map, encyclopedia, or another resource to fill in the missing bridge connections. (Hint: One of the bodies of water is used twice.)

Bridge Information

1. **George Washington Bridge**
   Body of water: _____
   Begins at: Fort Lee, New Jersey
   Ends at: New York City, New York

2. **Bayonne Bridge**
   Body of water: Kill Van Kull Channel
   Begins at: Bayonne, New Jersey
   Ends at: _____

3. **Benjamin Franklin Bridge**
   Body of water: _____
   Begins at: Gloucester City, New Jersey
   Ends at: Philadelphia, Pennsylvania

4. **Betsy Ross Bridge**
   Body of water: Delaware River
   Begins at: Pennsauken, New Jersey
   Ends at: _____

5. **Delaware Memorial Bridge**
   Body of water: _____
   Begins at: Pennsville, New Jersey
   Ends at: New Castle, Delaware

Missing Connections

Bodies of water
Delaware River
Hudson River

Ends at:
Philadelphia, PA
Staten Island, NY

Comprehension Questions

1. Jersey City is the capital of New Jersey.

   True or false? _____

2. Which of the following bodies of water is NOT important to New Jersey?

   A. Atlantic Ocean
   B. Delaware River
   C. Hudson River
   D. Missouri River

3. If you ranked all 50 states in size from 1st (largest) to 50th (smallest), what ranking would you give New Jersey?

   _____

4. In the sentence,
   "The 'Garden State' earned its nickname during the Revolutionary War for its ability to supply food to the colonies,"
   the word *earned* means _____.

   A. changed its name
   B. deserved because of doing something
   C. forced to take action
   D. was named in fun

5. New Jersey has a population density of approximately 1,100 people per square mile. The United States has an average population density of only 80 people per square mile. How many more people are in an average New Jersey square mile than in an average square mile? How many average square miles do you need to add together before you have more people than in a single New Jersey square mile? Explain.

   _____

   _____

   _____

NEW JERSEY

NEW MEXICO

State Facts

Nickname: _____

Became a State: _____

State Bird: _____

State Flower: _____

State Tree: _____

Fun Fact: _____

Isn't Manhattan in New York? Then, what was the top-secret Manhattan Project doing in New Mexico during World War II? Making atomic bombs, that's what. Scientists still work at the Los Alamos National Laboratory near Santa Fe, New Mexico. Today they research both military and non-military uses of *nuclear* (atomic) energy.

Native Americans lived in New Mexico tens of thousands of years before nuclear energy was discovered. Today's Pueblo Indians are descendants of the cliff-dwelling Anasazi people. Most live in Pueblo villages in northwestern New Mexico. Unlike other Native Americans, the Pueblo were never forced far from their homeland. The Navajo and Apache tribes were not so lucky. Many Navajo and Apache Indians live on reservations in New Mexico.

New Mexico is one of the largest states in the country. It's also one of the least populated. One-tenth of this population is American Indian. New Mexico came under Spanish and Mexican rule for more than three centuries. Santa Fe has been New Mexico's capital for almost 400 years!

In 1848, Mexico gave up this region to the United States. The railroad attracted cowboys and cattle ranchers to New Mexico. The discovery of silver and copper, then oil and natural gas, brought in miners. In 1912, New Mexico became the 47th state. New Mexico shares a portion of its southern border with the country of Mexico. Over one-third of all New Mexicans are *Hispanic* (a person of Latin-American descent). Visitors can see New Mexico's cultural history everywhere—at ancient Indian dwellings, colorful Spanish fiestas, and rodeos.

The Rocky Mountains reach into the central part of New Mexico. The rest of the state also lies high above sea level. In the east is America's Great Plains. In the west is a high plateau, filled with scattered mountains and deep canyons. The Rio Grande snakes down the center of the state. New Mexico relies on this river for much of its water.

New Mexico's climate is warm and dry, and has lots of sunshine. It's no wonder that the state flag pictures the ancient Zia Pueblo Indians' ancient symbol for the sun.

Mapping New Mexico's Spanish Heritage

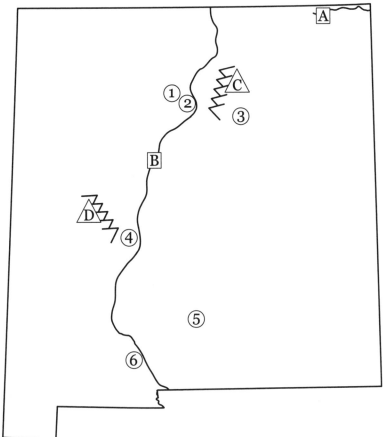

NEW MEXICO

Not until 1912 did New Mexico become the 47th state. Because the New Mexico area was under Spanish control for hundreds of years, many places in New Mexico have Spanish names. There are English translations of two rivers, two mountain ranges, and six cities listed below. Use an encyclopedia, a Spanish dictionary or another resource to help you write the Spanish name next to each English translation. Then, check an atlas to see if you translated correctly.

Rivers

A. Big River _____
B. Wild River _____

Mountains

C. Blood of Christ Mountains _____
_____

D. Hens Mountains _____
_____

Cities

1. The Cottonwood Trees _____
2. Holy Faith _____
3. The Meadows _____
4. Help _____
5. The Fat Cottonwood Tree _____
_____
6. The Crosses _____

Comprehension Questions

1. The Navajo are descendants of the native Anasazi people.

   True or false? _____

2. Which of the following is New Mexico's most important river?

   A. Alamosa River
   B. Mora River
   C. Rio Grande
   D. Rio Hondo

3. Approximately one-tenth of all New Mexicans are Native American. If there are 1,800,000 people living in New Mexico, how many of these people are Native American?

   _____

4. In the sentence,
   "New Mexico relies on this river for much of its water,"
   the word *relies* means _____.

   A. depends on
   B. drinks from
   C. looks to
   D. uses

5. Over one-third of all New Mexicans are Spanish-speaking. Considering New Mexico's history and location, why do you think so many people in New Mexico speak Spanish?

   _____

   _____

   _____

   _____

State Facts

Nickname: _____
Became a State: _____
State Bird: _____
State Flower: _____
State Tree: _____
Fun Fact: _____

In 1966, scientists in the Finger Lakes region of New York created a new apple. What did they call it? The Empire apple, of course. New York is, after all, the "Empire State." You can find the towering Empire State Building in the "Big Apple," New York City.

New York City is the largest city in the United States. It is the financial heart of the country. People from all over the world come here to work and live. How do you get to New York City? Just follow the Hudson River.

The Hudson River trickles out of the Adirondack Mountains in upstate New York. It flows south past the capital city of Albany, and through the Catskill Mountains. Miles later, the Hudson empties into the Atlantic Ocean at Long Island Sound. This is where you'll find Manhattan Island, Staten Island, and Long Island—all parts of the Big Apple. But there's another way to get to New York City. Just zip across the Atlantic. The Statue of Liberty in New York Harbor has welcomed immigrants from every corner of the world for over a century. Many of these immigrants stay in New York City.

The Atlantic Ocean and the Hudson River aren't the only bodies of water important to the Empire State. Two of the five Great Lakes, Lake Erie and Lake Ontario, border northern New York. These massive lakes are connected to the Atlantic Ocean by the St. Lawrence River. They are connected to each other by the Niagara River. This is where you can see Niagara Falls, one of the natural wonders of the world.

New York is a major publishing and clothing manufacturing state. Agriculture is also important. Dairy farms, fruit orchards, and vineyards are found throughout the state, even on Long Island. New York's orchards produce more apples than any other state except Washington. Half of the country's entire Empire apple crop is grown here. So, the next time you bite into a tart, juicy Empire apple, think of the Empire State.

NEW YORK

Ellis Island, Gateway to the New World

Ellis Island was called the "Gateway to the New World" because it was the first stop for people arriving at New York Harbor. Between 1820 and 1890, millions of immigrants left their homelands and were ready to start their new lives in America.

Use the following information to determine the total number of immigrants that came from each of the listed countries during those 70 years. Calculate your answers on a separate sheet of paper.

NEW YORK

A. Austria-Hungary: 460,000 immigrants   460,000

B. England: 5 times the number from Austria-Hungary   _____

C. Norway & Sweden: 2 times the number from Austria-Hungary   _____

D. Italy: 45,000 less than the number from Austria-Hungary _____

E. Russia & Poland: 110,000 less than the number from Austria-Hungary _____

F. China: 20,000 less than the number from Norway & Sweden,
                      divided by 3
                      (_____ - 20,000) / 3 =   _____

G. Ireland: The sum of the immigrants from England, Norway
                      & Sweden, and China
                      _____ + _____ + _____ =   _____

H. Switzerland: Half the number from Russia & Poland
                      _____ / 2 =   _____

I. Denmark: Half the number from China
                      _____ / 2 =   _____

J. France: 3 times the number from Switzerland,
                      minus the number from Denmark
                      (3 x _____) - _____ =   _____

According to this information, the most immigrants came from   _____.

and the fewest immigrants came from   _____.

Comprehension Questions

1. New York City is on the Hudson River.

   True or false? _____

2. Where does the Hudson River begin its journey to the sea?

   A. Adirondack Mountains
   B. Catskill Mountains
   C. Lake Erie
   D. Lake Ontario

3. Name two major New York cities:

   _____   _____

4. In the sentence,
   "So, the next time you bite into a tart, juicy Empire apple, think of the Empire State,"
   the word *tart* means _____.

   A. green
   B. red
   C. sour
   D. sweet

5. Legend has it that President George Washington gave New York State the nickname of "Empire State." What is an empire? Why do you think Washington called New York state an empire?

   _____

   _____

   _____

   _____

NEW YORK

State Facts

Nickname: _____

Became a State: _____

State Bird: _____

State Flower: _____

State Tree: _____

Fun Fact: _____

Since before the Civil War, North Carolina has produced more tobacco than any other state. Tobacco manufacturing employs many people. But this isn't why the beautiful mountains that separate North Carolina from Tennessee are called The Great Smokies. Mist swirls around the mountains' forested peaks.

The Great Smoky Mountains are part of the Blue Ridge Mountains that run through western North Carolina. These mountains form a small portion of the 1,500-mile-long Appalachian Mountain system. North Carolina's Mount Mitchell is the highest point in the entire Appalachians. However, mountains cover only the western fifth of the state.

Most of the state's population lives in central North Carolina. This slightly hilly land is called the Piedmont Plateau. This is where big cities such as Charlotte, Greensboro, Winston-Salem, and Raleigh, the capital, are located. This is where you'll find North Carolina's industries: tobacco manufacturing, chemical manufacturing, textiles, electronics, and furniture-making. One-third of the state is farmland; the rest is forest. Chances are that some of your wooden furniture was made in North Carolina.

Mountains are in the west and the plateau is in the center, but what's in the east? The swampy Atlantic Coastal Plain and 300 miles of ocean coast. Including all the islands, reefs, and sand bars, North Carolina has more than 3,300 miles of tidal coastline. Sailors, beware! The rough coast here has caused more shipwrecks than anywhere else in the world. Cape Hatteras, off the northeastern coast, is called the "Graveyard of the Atlantic." For this reason, lighthouses are a prominent feature of the coastline.

North Carolina's coast offers other mysteries besides shipwrecks. How about the "Mystery of the Lost Colony?" English settlers first colonized Roanoke Island in 1587. Within three years, all of the inhabitants had completely disappeared. Then, there is the "Mystery of Flight." At least, it was a mystery until 1903. That's when the Wright Brothers, Orville and Wilbur, came to North Carolina from Ohio to make their first successful airplane flight at Kitty Hawk, on North Carolina's Outer Banks.

Digging for Treasure

A ferocious pirate known as Blackbeard terrorized the seas along the Virginia and South Carolina coast. Blackbeard's favorite hideout was an island in North Carolina's Outer Banks. He was captured and killed there in 1718, but his treasure was never recovered. Follow this trail of treasure to find out the name of the island Blackbeard called home!

There are eight North Carolina towns marked with numbered treasure bags on the map below. These town are listed alphabetically in the Treasure Towns list. Beside these names is the list of numbered treasure bags.

Use a map, encyclopedia, or another resource to match each numbered treasure bag with the correct North Carolina Treasure Town. Write the matching town names in the spaces provided beside each treasure bag. (Hint: You won't use all of the spaces.)

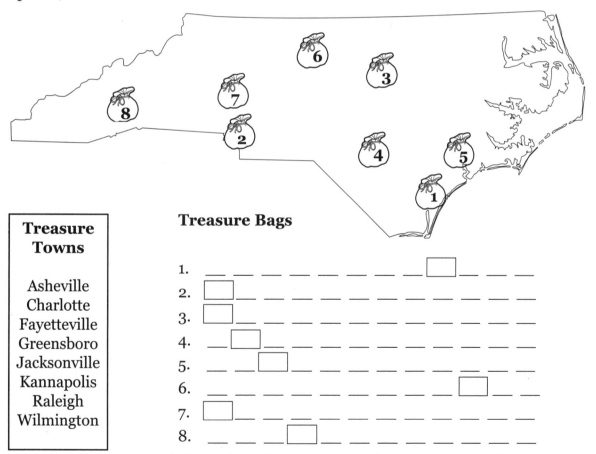

Treasure Towns

Asheville
Charlotte
Fayetteville
Greensboro
Jacksonville
Kannapolis
Raleigh
Wilmington

Treasure Bags

1. __ __ __ __ __ __ [ ] __ __ __
2. [ ] __ __ __ __ __ __ __ __
3. [ ] __ __ __ __ __ __ __ __
4. __ [ ] __ __ __ __ __ __
5. __ __ [ ] __ __ __ __ __ __
6. __ __ __ __ __ __ __ [ ] __ __
7. [ ] __ __ __ __ __ __
8. __ __ __ [ ] __ __ __ __ __ __ __

When you have completed matching the towns with the treasure bags, the boxed letters, in order, will spell out the name of Blackbeard's island hideout.

___ ___ ___ ___ ___ ___ ___ ___ Island

Comprehension Questions

1. The Great Smoky Mountains are part of the Appalachian Mountains.

   True or false? _____

2. Which of the following cities is the capital of North Carolina?

   A. Charlotte
   B. Greensboro
   C. Kitty Hawk
   D. Raleigh

3. Which section of North Carolina is mountainous: east, central, or west?

   _____

4. In the sentence,
   "Tobacco manufacturing employs many people,"
   the word *employs* means _____.

   A. commonly
   B. factory
   C. provides money for
   D. provides work for

5. The Great Smoky Mountains are named for the layers of haze that often cloak the mountain peaks. How do you think the Blue Ridge Mountains got their name?

   _____

   _____

   _____

   _____

   _____

   _____

CD-0774 50 States

NORTH CAROLINA

State Facts

Nickname: _____

Became a State: _____

State Bird: _____

State Flower: _____

State Tree: _____

Fun Fact: _____

NORTH DAKOTA

If you stood in the middle of North America and planted some grain beneath your feet, would it grow? You bet! The geographic center of the entire continent lies in a small agricultural town in North Dakota. North Dakota produces more barley, rye, flax, and spring wheat than any other state.

Why is the soil here so fertile? Two major rivers feed North Dakota. The Red River of the North runs along the state's eastern border with Minnesota. Two of the largest cities, Fargo and Grand Forks, are located on the banks of this river. Most North Dakotans live in the fertile Red River Valley. Flooding is common. The other main river is the Missouri, which cuts across western North Dakota. Bismarck, the capital, and historic Fort Mandan lie along this river. The Lewis and Clark Expedition built this fort in 1804, on their journey to the Pacific Ocean.

Before white settlement, North Dakota's plains were covered in prairie grass. Ojibwe and Sioux Indians hunted buffalo on the plains. The Mandan, Hidatsa, and other tribes farmed along the Missouri. When the railroad arrived, so did the settlers. Americans moved west, along with immigrants from Germany, Norway, and other Scandinavian countries. The Indians were forced onto reservations and great herds of buffalo were destroyed. Today, almost all of North Dakota's flat, rich land is used for growing crops or grazing cattle. There are few cities. Most manufacturing relies on agriculture. The only place where you won't see wheat is in the southwest, in an area called the Badlands. The Badlands are made of soft, sedimentary rock that has been eroded into fantastic shapes throughout the centuries.

So, think of North Dakota when you're eating your breakfast cereal, your lunchtime sandwich, your dinner of beef-and-barley soup, and when you're munching on those salty seed snacks during your baseball game. That's right, North Dakota is also the country's top producer of sunflowers!

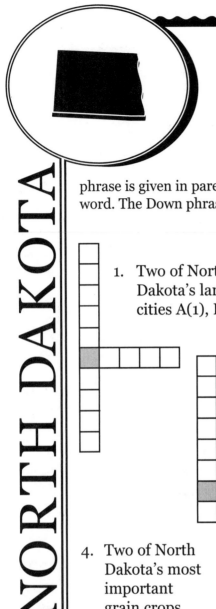

Crossing North Dakota

Each of these six mini-crossword puzzles contains two related words or phrases. Each numbered puzzle pair has at least one letter in common. This is the boxed letter. Use the clues listed below to complete the puzzles. (Hint: You'll have to figure out which phrase goes across and which phrase goes down in each puzzle. The number of words in the phrase is given in parentheses. For example: Puzzle #1, A(1), D(2). The Across phrase has one word. The Down phrase has two words.)

1. Two of North Dakota's largest cities A(1), D(2)

2. A national park in western North Dakota is named for this popular president. A(1), D(1)

3. These two officers, ____ and ____, led the 1803 expedition to the Pacific Ocean. They wintered at Fort Mandan, in central North Dakota. A(2), D(2)

4. Two of North Dakota's most important grain crops are: A(1), D(1)

5. North Dakota borders these two Canadian provinces. A(1), D(1)

6. North Dakota's state bird and state flower A(2), D(3)

The boxed letters of these six puzzles, unscrambled, will spell out the English translation of the Sioux word "Dakota."

___ ___ ___ ___ ___ ___

Comprehension Questions

1. Minnesota is east of North Dakota.

   True or false? _____

2. Where are the Badlands of North Dakota located?

   A. in the northeast
   B. in the northwest
   C. in the southeast
   D. in the southwest

3. Where did Meriwether Lewis and William Clark spend the winter of 1804?

   _____

4. In the sentence,
   "Americans moved west, along with immigrants from Germany, Norway, and other Scandinavian countries,"
   the word *immigrants* means _____.

   A. farmers
   B. people who come into a new country to live
   C. people who come into a new country to visit
   D. travelers

5. Three of North Dakota's four main cities (Bismarck, Fargo, and Grand Forks) lie on the Missouri River or the Red River of the North. Why?

   _____

   _____

   _____

   _____

   _____

NORTH DAKOTA

OHIO

State Facts

Nickname: _____
Became a State: _____
State Bird: _____
State Flower: _____
State Tree: _____
Fun Fact: _____

What is it about Ohio that has given us seven American Presidents? Is it something in the water? Maybe. There's plenty of water in Ohio. Lake Erie, one of the Great Lakes, lies along Ohio's northern border. This gives Ohio access to the Atlantic Ocean. The Ohio River is a major *tributary* (arm) of the Mississippi River. This tributary runs along Ohio's borders with West Virginia and Kentucky. Many of Ohio's first white settlers floated down the Ohio River to reach their new homes. The Ohio River has provided waterpower for industries since the Industrial Revolution.

Maybe there's something in Ohio's soil that has created so many presidents. The soil in western Ohio is particularly fertile. Half of the state is farmland. Corn and soybeans are Ohio's most important crops. What if you look under the soil? You'll probably find salt—enough salt to supply the entire country for more than a *millennium* (1,000 years)! In eastern Ohio, you'll find coal. Coal is a very important natural resource for many industries, too.

Perhaps the reason so many presidents have come from Ohio is because of Ohio's population. Only six other states are more populated, although 33 states are larger in size. Therefore, Ohio's chances of producing a president are better than most states! Three-quarters of these people live in cities. Ohio has some of the most important manufacturing cities in the nation. Columbus (the capital), Cleveland, Cincinnati, Toledo, and Akron are only some of Ohio's industrial centers. Workers in these cities make thousands of different products, including cars, machinery, plastics, and steel.

Maybe the number of presidents from Ohio has something to do with transportation. Ohio became the 17th state in 1803. At that time, Ohio was the westernmost state in the nation. People used Ohio's rivers and lakes as highways for themselves and their goods. Eventually they added man-made canals, railroad tracks, and roads. Transportation became easier than ever.

Whatever the reason, those seven Ohio-born presidents would probably agree on two things: it took a lot of hard work to get them to the White House, and more than a little luck.

Ohio's Famous People

Seven American presidents were born in Ohio. Many other famous people were born there, too. Below are two lists; the first is a list of famous people from Ohio, and the second is a list of their accomplishments.

Use an encyclopedia or another resource to match these famous people with their accomplishments. Write the famous person's corresponding letter next to the matching accomplishment. Check off the names as you go along.

A. Neil Armstrong

B. Thomas Edison

C. James Garfield

D. John Glenn

E. Ulysses S. Grant

F. Warren G. Harding

G. Benjamin Harrison

H. Rutherford B. Hayes

I. William McKinley

J. Jack Nicklaus

K. Annie Oakley

L. Steven Spielberg

M. R. L. Stine

N. William Taft

O. Tecumseh

P. Victoria Woodhull

Q. Orville Wright

_____ 1. *Goosebumps* series author

_____ 2. 1st woman to run for president (in 1872)

_____ 3. 18th President of the United States

_____ 4. 19th President of the United States

_____ 5. 20th President of the United States

_____ 6. 23rd President of the United States

_____ 7. 25th President of the United States

_____ 8. 27th President of the United States

_____ 9. 29th President of the United States

_____ 10. Film director

_____ 11. Co-inventor of first successful airplane

_____ 12. American professional golfer

_____ 13. First American astronaut to orbit the Earth

_____ 14. First person to walk on the moon

_____ 15. Inventor of the lightbulb

_____ 16. Shawnee Indian chief

_____ 17. Wild West sharpshooter

Comprehension Questions

1. Ohio's most important crop is tobacco.

   True or false? _____

2. The Ohio River is a tributary of which of the following rivers?

   A. the Delaware River
   B. the Hudson River
   C. the Mississippi River
   D. the Missouri River

3. How many states had joined the Union before Ohio joined?

   _____

4. In the sentence,
   "This gives Ohio access to the Atlantic Ocean,"
   the word *access* means _____.

   A. a closing
   B. a shipping path
   C. a river route to
   D. a way of getting to

5. Ohio has a large enough supply of salt to last for 1,000 years. A decade is 10 years. A century is 100 years. What do we call 1,000 years? How many centuries are in 1,000 years? How many decades are in 1,000 years?

   _____

   _____

   _____

   _____

   _____

Nickname: _____
Became a State: _____
State Bird: _____
State Flower: _____
State Tree: _____
Fun Fact: _____

OKLAHOMA

Grab a ruler and start measuring! Oklahoma lies as far from the Pacific Ocean as it does from the Atlantic Ocean. But if you look closely, you will see that the *panhandle* (narrow strip of land) in the northwestern corner is pointing west. West was the direction traders journeyed along the Santa Fe Trail. West was the direction white settlers followed in their search for more land. West was also the direction the Five Civilized Tribes traveled when forced onto the "Trail of Tears."

Most of Oklahoma was originally called Indian Territory. Indian Territory continuously shrank in size after being created in 1834. Eager settlers rushing to claim land sooner than the official 1889 opening of the smaller Oklahoma Territory gave the state its nickname, the "Sooner State." Indian Territory disappeared in 1907 when it merged with Oklahoma to become the 46th state. More than 50 Native American tribes still live in Oklahoma. This is the greatest concentration of Native Americans in the country. Tribes from the Great Plains, such as the Southern Cheyenne and Osage, as well as the Five Civilized Tribes (Chickasaw, Cherokee, Choctaw, Creek, and Seminole) and other displaced tribes, all call Oklahoma home.

Oklahoma is part of America's Great Plains. Cattle graze and crops grow well. Only in the far east do you find higher, more rugged hills. Irrigation systems have created hundreds of man-made lakes. Oil wells are everywhere. Tornadoes and dust storms are common in the warm climate.

The three kings of Oklahoma are cattle, wheat, and oil. Oklahoma is an enormous producer of fuel and food. Even the capitol building in Oklahoma City was built over an oil well. The Arkansas River in northeastern Oklahoma feeds into the Mississippi River, which empties into the Gulf of Mexico. Dams along the Arkansas River have allowed the oil city of Tulsa to become an important inland "seaport."

Oklahoma's location at the nation's heart is perfect for transporting products all over the country. On a map, Oklahoma still points west. However, people living in all parts of the country benefit from Oklahoma's riches.

OKLAHOMA

Learn more about the state of Oklahoma. Use a dictionary, encyclopedia, or atlas to help you fill in the blanks in the sentences below. Each of the missing words starts with the corresponding letter in the name Oklahoma.

O Cowboy humorist Will Rogers was born near O __ __ __ __ __ __, Oklahoma, in 1879. He liked to boast of his Cherokee Indian heritage by saying, "My ancestors may not have come over on the Mayflower, but they met 'em at the boat."

K The Cheyenne people resisted the government's attempts to place them on a reservation. Cheyenne Chief Black K __ __ __ __ __ survived an 1864 massacre at Sand Creek, Colorado, only to be killed four years later when Lieutenant Colonel George Custer's troops attacked the tribe near Cheyenne, Oklahoma.

L Known to English-speakers as the Delaware Indians, the L __ __ __- __ __ __ __ __ __ ("original people") were gradually driven westward from their lands along the Delaware River to present-day Oklahoma.

A In 1830, President Andrew Jackson approved the Indian Removal A __ __. This resulted in the forced relocation of thousands of American Indians to lands west of the Mississippi River. The Five Civilized Tribes of America's southeast sometimes refer to this relocation march as the "Trail of Tears."

H President Benjamin H __ __ __ __ __ __ __ __ declared the unassigned American Indian lands of Oklahoma open for settlement on April 22, 1889. At noon that day, Oklahoma City was just a lonely prairie railroad stop. By sundown, it had blossomed into a tent city of over 10,000 people.

O A group of World War I Chocktaw soldiers (code talkers) used their native language to encode secret military messages, saving their battalion from defeat. The name Oklahoma comes from the Chocktaw language: *O* __ __ __ means people, *humma* means red.

M The M __ __ __ __ __ __ __ __ __ is Oklahoma's state flower.

A The home of Cherokee Indian Sequoya, creator of the Cherokee a __ __ __ __ __ __ __ and namesake of the Giant Sequoia tree, can still be seen near Sallisaw, Oklahoma.

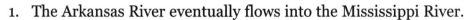

Comprehension Questions

1. The Arkansas River eventually flows into the Mississippi River.

   True or false? _____

2. Which of the following is NOT one of the original Five Civilized Tribes?

   A. Cherokee
   B. Chickasaw
   C. Seminole
   D. Southern Cheyenne

3. What is the name of the narrow strip of land found in northern Oklahoma?

   _____

4. In the sentence,
   "Tribes from the Great Plains, such as the Southern Cheyenne and Osage, as well as
   the Five Civilized Tribes (the Chickasaw, Cherokee, Choctaw, Creek, and Seminole)
   and other displaced tribes all call Oklahoma home,"
   the word *displaced* means _____.

   A. civilized
   B. forced from their home
   C. eager to move
   D. wandering

5. In the text, Tulsa is called an inland seaport. Why is this a good description?

   _____

   _____

   _____

   _____

   _____

OKLAHOMA

OREGON

State Facts

Nickname: _____

Became a State: _____

State Bird: _____

State Flower: _____

State Tree: _____

Fun Fact: _____

In the mid-1800s, thousands of people trudged westward along the Oregon Trail. Many of these adventurers never made it to Oregon. Some turned back; some died along the way. Others split off to California. The rest ended up in Oregon—America's Pacific Wonderland. They joined Native American tribes such as the Chinook, Kalapuya, Klamath, and Nez Perce, who had lived in Oregon for centuries. Many modern Oregonians can trace their ancestors back to that difficult journey. Those pioneers played an important role in expanding the nation "from sea to shining sea."

Oregon ends at the Pacific Ocean. Mountain ranges guard the coast. The Columbia River meets the Pacific Ocean in the northwestern corner of the state. This is where the Lewis and Clark Expedition spent the winter after finally reaching the sea. High and rugged as these coastal mountains are, they're no match for the huge Cascade Range found inland.

The Cascades split Oregon into two sections: the dry east and the wet west. The larger section east of the Cascades is where you'll find most of Oregon's cattle ranches. Irrigation here allows farmers to grow crops such as wheat. The smaller section west of the Cascades includes some of the state's most fertile land. The Willamette River flows through much of this section. This valley is filled with fruit orchards and vineyards. Oregon's biggest cities are located here, including Salem, the capital, and Portland.

Although the Cascade Range is volcanic, none of Oregon's volcanoes are currently active. They used to be! Oregon's Crater Lake is the deepest lake in the country. It was formed several thousand years ago when Mount Mazama, a now-extinct volcano, collapsed. Mount Hood is Oregon's highest peak. It last erupted in 1865.

Trees are more important to Oregon than cattle, apples, and wheat put together. Forests cover half of the state. Much of Oregon's manufacturing relies on wood and wood products. However, Oregon doesn't just cut down trees. Foresters work to find other ways to conserve Oregon's greatest natural resource. Specialists are always developing new uses for the *by-products* (leftovers) of the forestry industry.

Following Directions to Oregon

The Oregon Trail covered over 2,000 miles. It took travelers up to six months to reach their new homes. Staying on the path was extremely important. One wrong turn, and they might be lost forever. These adventurers had to make sure that they followed their directions exactly.

Dr. John McLoughlin was one of the first people to greet these new settlers. McLoughlin was a fur-trader with the British-Canadian Hudson's Bay Company. He helped "overlanders" get settled by giving them food and goods. He also gave the newcomers advice regarding where they might find the best available land. McLoughlin eventually became an American citizen. He founded Oregon City, Oregon's first state capital, and served as mayor for several years.

Today, the name *John McLoughlin* is a state symbol. Starting with the name *John McLoughlin*, carefully follow the directions below to discover this man's official state title. (Hint: Each direction applies to the new "word" or "phrase" that you have just made.) Don't be fooled! These "words" may not make sense until you solve the puzzle.

JOHN MCLOUGHLIN

1. _____ 1. Change all the L's to T's

2. _____ 2. Switch the 11th and 12th letters

3. _____ 3. Replace "TO" with "FROM"

4. _____ 4. Move the last four letters, in order, to the beginning

5. _____ 5. Change all the M's to E's

6. _____ 6. Delete the 7th consonant

7. _____ 7. Reverse the 11th and 12th letters

8. _____ 8. Replace "THIN JOHN" with "FAT RON"

9. _____ 9. Move the 5th and 6th letters, in order, to the end

10. _____ 10. Switch the 4th and 5th letters

11. _____ 11. Double the first O

12. _____ 12. Move the 11th letter to the 4th position

13. _____ 13. Reverse the 7th and 8th letters

14. _____ 14. Replace the 2nd vowel with an H

John McLoughlin is known as the

" __ __ __ __ __ __ __ __ __ __ __ __ __ __ __ __ ."

Comprehension Questions

1. The Willamette Indians were a tribe native to Oregon.

    True or false? _____

2. Which of the following cities is the capital of Oregon?

    A. Olympia
    B. Oregon City
    C. Portland
    D. Salem

3. The Cascade Range divides the state of Oregon into two sections. Which section is smaller—the land to the east of these mountains, or the land to the west of these mountains?

    _____

4. In the sentence,
    "Foresters work to find other ways to conserve Oregon's greatest natural resource."
    the word *conserve* means _____.

    A. exploit
    B. supply
    C. avoid wasteful use of
    D. redistribute

5. In what way(s) do you think the forestry industry could help with conservation efforts?

    _____

    _____

    _____

    _____

    _____

    _____

State Facts

Nickname: _____
Became a State: _____
State Bird: _____
State Flower: _____
State Tree: _____
Fun Fact: _____

Pennsylvania is all about history. "HIS-story" may be the story of William Penn, Pennsylvania's founder. King Charles II of England gave Penn this huge piece of land in 1681. Penn was a member of a religious group called the Quakers. Quakers are *pacifists* (opposed to war). Penn created the city of Philadelphia as a center of religious freedom. *Philadelphia* means "Brotherly Love."

Perhaps "HIS-story" is the story of General George Washington. Washington's troops were defeated by the British at the Battles of Brandywine and Germantown, both in Pennsylvania. The following winter, the American army nearly froze to death in Valley Forge, near Philadelphia. The Americans eventually won the Revolutionary War. George Washington went on to become the new country's first president.

Maybe we should say that the "Keystone State" is all about "IT-story." "It" was the signing of the Declaration of Independence and the acceptance of the United States Constitution. "It" was also the Civil War's bloody Battle of Gettysburg and President Abraham Lincoln's emotional Gettysburg Address.

Pennsylvania has "HER-story," too. According to legend, seamstress Betsy Ross of Philadelphia sewed the first American flag—the red, white, and blue Stars and Stripes. Biologist Rachel Carson, born near the giant steel town of Pittsburgh, is considered to be the "Mother of the Environmental Movement."

Pennsylvania also has a lot of "THEIR-story." "They" were the immigrants who came to Pennsylvania. At first, they came for religious freedom. The Pennsylvania Dutch today are people who can trace their roots back to those early German immigrants. Many operate dairy farms in eastern Pennsylvania. Some, such as the Amish and Mennonites, live very simply, without modern inventions. Later, more immigrants came in search of work. Pennsylvania has enormous deposits of coal. Many large rivers, including the Ohio, the Delaware, and the Susquehanna, have helped Pennsylvania develop into a major industrial state. Both Pittsburgh and Philadelphia are important manufacturing centers. The immigrants of yesterday are the Americans of today.

Any way you look at Pennsylvania's history, one thing is certain. Pennsylvania's history is "our story," the story of the United States of America.

Ringing in Independence

On July 8, 1776, one day after the Thirteen Colonies declared independence from Britain, bells rang out all over America.

Listed in the Word Bank below are some words and phrases important to Pennsylvania. Find and cross out each of these words in the puzzle. (Hint: Names with more than one word will be found separately in the Pride of Pennsylvania puzzle. For example, Betsy will be separate from Ross.) Do not find the category labels.

Word Bank

People
Amish
Benjamin Franklin
Betsy Ross
James Buchanan
Louisa May Alcott
Mennonites
Robert Peary
William Penn

Places
Brandywine
Mount Davis
Philadelphia
Valley Forge

Economy
chocolate
coal
iron
steel

Borders
Lake Erie
Maryland
New York
West Virginia

Pride of Pennsylvania

```
A A L C I Y Y Z Y Q E W Y A E R C
I L M S O R E U C N E S S G C E W
B M C I P A O M A N T I R L J O G
E A M O S H L N I E U O E E Y H F
M Y R I T H I W B O F E K L G U R
A T S Y H T Y L L T T A N O D W A
R Y J A S D M M A S L A P Y M E N
Y B T R N A D G E D E B P E R S K
L E V A I Y Y S Z N E P J E N T L
A L R L E L K E U X N L D A A N I
N B L L T L F D X V I O P A M R N
D I L N B N E H Z Q Q R N H V E Y
W A U E J E A C Y O R K O I I I S
V O I S V I R G I N I A K B T A S
M R S Z P W B U C H A N A N E E I
E O B E N J A M I N P E D V J R S
R G P H G I O C H O C O L A T E T
```

The most famous of these bells that rang on Independence Day hung in Philadelphia's Independence Hall. In the top eleven horizontal rows, circle the first unused letter. These letters, in order, will spell out the name of this famous bell:

__ __ __ __ __ __ __ __ __ __

Comprehension Questions

1. William Penn was against war.

   True or false? _____

2. Which of the following battles was NOT fought in Pennsylvania?

   A. Battle of Bunker Hill
   B. Battle of Brandywine
   C. Battle of Germantown
   D. Battle of Gettysburg

3. Name an important river in Pennsylvania.

   _____

4. In the sentence,
   "The Pennsylvania Dutch today are people who can trace their roots back to those early German immigrants,"
   the word *roots* means _____.

   A. ancestors
   B. farmers
   C. gardening
   D. German

5. Pennsylvania was one of the original Thirteen Colonies. It is sometimes called the "Keystone State." Considering Pennsylvania's history, why do you think this name is appropriate? What other reason might there be? (Look at a map for help.)

   _____

   _____

   _____

   _____

PENNSYLVANIA

RHODE ISLAND

State Facts

Nickname: _____
Became a State: _____
State Bird: _____
State Flower: _____
State Tree: _____
Fun Fact: _____

The New England state of Rhode Island fits between Massachusetts and Connecticut. This state isn't even 50 miles wide, but its Atlantic shoreline measures almost 500 miles. That's because most of the state is island. Aquidneck Island (the real "Rhode Island") is the largest of over 30 islands in the state. These islands, plus the mainland surrounding Narragansett Bay, form the State of Rhode Island and Providence Plantations. Rhode Island is so tiny it could fit into Alaska 400 times!

The first non-native settlers came to Rhode Island in 1636. Colonist Roger Williams and his supporters had been banished from Massachusetts because of religious differences. Williams founded the town of Providence, the state capital, on Narragansett Bay, with land purchased from the Narragansett Indians. Other religious and political Massachusetts *exiles* (people forced to leave their community) followed. They created their own colonies on nearby Block Island and Aquidneck Island. Within 30 years, Williams had united these colonies under the name Rhode Island and Providence Plantations. War broke out between the settlers and the Native American tribes, including the Wampanoags. The war in 1675 ended with the death of the Wampanoag *sachem* (chief), who was called King Philip. With his death, Native American resistance to white settlers in New England ended.

Sandy beaches and salt ponds cover the land close to Narragansett Bay. Waves crash against island cliffs. The rocky uplands in the northwest do not rise more than 800 feet above sea level. Rhode Island enjoys milder weather than the other New England states. It is also harder hit by hurricanes.

Rhode Island is one of the original Thirteen Colonies. It was the first to declare itself independent from Britain in 1776. Its jewelry and *textile* (clothing and material) industries, so important in the last two centuries, remain strong today. But strongest is the ocean. From shipbuilding to fishing and sailing—in Rhode Island, you are never far from the sea.

R...H...O...D...E I...S...L...A...N...D

Learn more about the state of Rhode Island. Use a dictionary, encyclopedia, or atlas to help you fill in the blanks in the sentences below. Each of the missing words starts with the corresponding letter in the name Rhode Island.

R   Although Rhode Island was the first colony to declare independence in 1776, it was the last of the original Thirteen Colonies to r __ __ __ __ __ (approve) the Constitution.

H   Rhode Island's state motto is H __ __ __.

O   After a victorious battle against the British on Lake Erie during the War of 1812, Rhode Island sailor O __ __ __ __ __ Hazard Perry told his military commander, "we have met the enemy, and they are ours."

D   Rhode Island's constitution remained unchanged until 1842, when the D __ __ __ Rebellion forced the acceptance of a more democratic and fair constitution.

E   In 1614, Dutch explorer Adriaen Block sighted Aquidneck Island and called it "Red Island," *Roodt E* __ __ __ __ __ __ in Dutch, because of the red clay he saw along the shore. Perhaps that is why it is called "Rhode Island" today.

I   Samuel Slater was the first person in America to build a water-powered spinning machine. This machine, first used in a Pawtucket mill, jump-started Rhode Island's textile industry. This was an important early step in America's own I __ __ __ __ __ __ __ __ __ Revolution.

S   The S __ __ __ __ __ __ __ River, running between Aquidneck Island and Rhode Island's eastern mainland, is actually a saltwater extension of Narragansett Bay.

L   David Melville, a inventor from Newport, received the first American gas l __ __ __ __ patent on March 24, 1810.

A   Anne Hutchinson and a group of her followers established the city of Pocasset (now Portsmouth), Rhode Island, in 1638. Hutchinson belonged to a group called the A __ __ __ __ __ __ __ __ __ __ , who were exiled from Massachusetts for their religious beliefs.

N   The summer resort town of N __ __ __ __ __ __ was an important shipbuilding town. It was host to the America's Cup, the world-famous sailboat competition, for many years. This town remains a strong naval center today.

D   The D __ __ __ __ Brothers, Nehemiah and Seril, of Providence, Rhode Island, started up the jewelry industry in 1794.

Comprehension Questions

RHODE ISLAND

1. Roger Williams originally settled in Massachusetts.

   True or false? _____

2. What is the name of the capital of Rhode Island?

   A. Aquidneck
   B. Narragansett
   C. Providence
   D. Williamstown

3. What is another name for Aquidneck Island?

   _____

4. In the sentence,
   "Colonist Roger Williams and his supporters had been banished from Massachusetts because of religious differences,"
   the word *banished* means _____.

   A. living in
   B. running away
   C. sent away
   D. visiting

5. The earliest Rhode Island settlers were seeking more freedom, both religious and political. During the Revolutionary War, Rhode Island declared independence from Britain before any other state. Do you think there might be a connection between these two facts? What might that connection be?

   _____

   _____

   _____

   _____

State Facts

Nickname: _____

Became a State: _____

State Bird: _____

State Flower: _____

State Tree: _____

Fun Fact: _____

If you're a golfer, then South Carolina is the place for you. There are hundreds of golf courses in the eastern lowland near the Atlantic Ocean. Golf is just one of the many things tourists and residents love about South Carolina. The warm climate and beautiful beaches are big attractions as well.

South Carolina wasn't always a golfer's paradise. Before Europeans arrived, many different Native American tribes lived here. The Catawba, Cherokee, and Yamasee Indians were too busy farming to golf. By 1670, white settlers had moved in, mostly along the coast. These people farmed, too. Many of today's golfing greens used to be rice *paddies* (wet fields). As the rice plantations grew, so did the number of slaves working on the plantations. At the start of the Civil War, slaves made up over half of the state's population.

South Carolina was one of the original Thirteen Colonies. It was the most powerful of the states in the Deep South, although it was the smallest. The port city of Charleston was an important link in overseas trade with England. South Carolina was the first of the Confederate States to *secede* (break away) from the Union. The first shots of the Civil War were fired at Fort Sumter in Charleston. Union victory in the Civil War ended slavery. It also ended South Carolina's rice industry. Farmers today grow tobacco, cotton, and soybeans, and raise chickens and beef cattle. Fishermen haul in shrimp. However, manufacturing (chemicals and textiles) makes more money for the state than agriculture.

Even if you don't golf, there's a lot to do in South Carolina. Visitors enjoy the holiday resorts in Myrtle Beach, and walk the endless sandy beaches of the Grand Strand along the Atlantic. Visit the capital city of Columbia—a city that was burned to the ground during the Civil War. Or head for the Blue Ridge Mountains, which extend into the northwest corner of the state.

South Carolina offers a chance to see many different kinds of wildlife. Whales, sharks, and giant sea turtles swim offshore. Water birds, such as the Great Blue Heron and the Snowy Egret, can be seen wading in shallow water. Squirrels and foxes hide in thick inland forests. And look—is that an alligator sunning itself near the ninth hole?

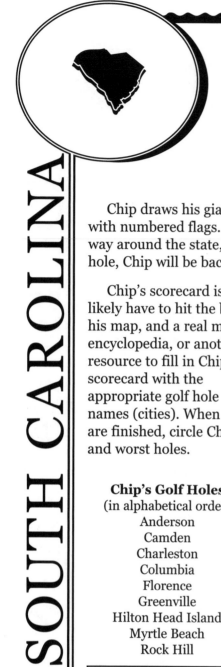

SOUTH CAROLINA

Golfing in South Carolina

A giant named Chip is vacationing in South Carolina. He wants to play some golf, but all of the courses are too small. Chip decides to make his own golf course. He chooses nine South Carolina cities as his nine holes, and adds water hazards (rivers, lakes, and an ocean).

Chip draws his giant golf course on a map of South Carolina. The holes (cities) are labeled with numbered flags. He places the clubhouse at Columbia. He will start here and work his way around the state, trying to hit a golf ball into all nine holes. When he finishes the ninth hole, Chip will be back at the clubhouse.

Chip's scorecard is shown below. The par column indicates how many times a player will likely have to hit the ball before the ball lands in the hole. Use Chip's list of golf holes (cities), his map, and a real map, encyclopedia, or another resource to fill in Chip's scorecard with the appropriate golf hole names (cities). When you are finished, circle Chip's best and worst holes.

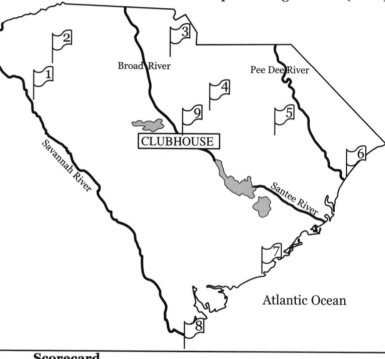

Chip's Golf Holes
(in alphabetical order)
Anderson
Camden
Charleston
Columbia
Florence
Greenville
Hilton Head Island
Myrtle Beach
Rock Hill

Name: Chip		Par	Score	Scorecard
Hole		Par	Score	Notes
1	_____	4	5	I overshot the first hole and ended up in the Savannah River.
2	_____	3	1	A hole in one—what a perfect shot!
3	_____	3	3	I barely hit the ball over the Broad River. I scored a par.
4	_____	3	2	Another good hole. My first *birdie* (one point under par).
5	_____	3	4	Watch out for the railroad tracks here.
6	_____	4	2	I crossed the Pee Dee River and scored my first *eagle* (two strokes under par).
7	_____	4	7	The beach was great! But, I went on to lose two balls on this hole—one in the Pee Dee and another in the Santee River.
8	_____	5	8	What a tough hole! I lost five balls just getting out to the island!
9	_____	6	4	Scored another eagle! A wonderful way to end my game!
Total		35	36	Just one stroke over par—not bad for a giant!

CD-0774 50 States

Comprehension Questions

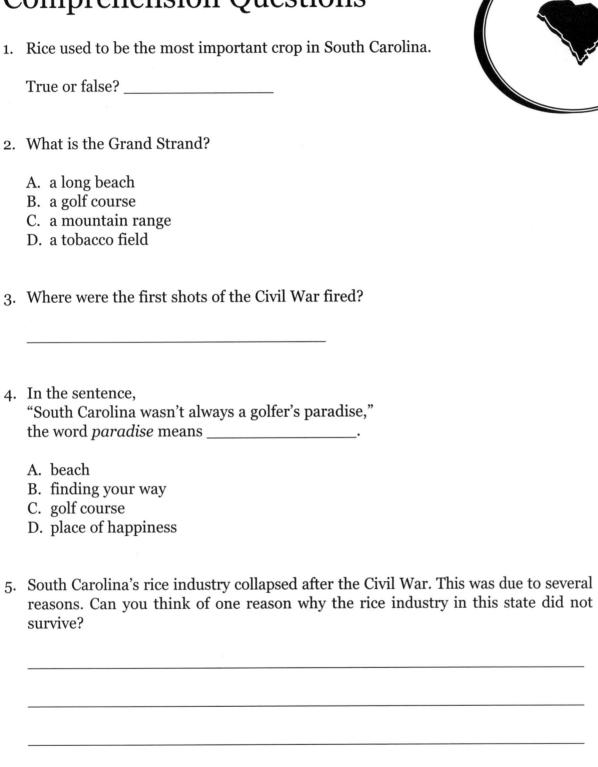

1. Rice used to be the most important crop in South Carolina.

   True or false? _____

2. What is the Grand Strand?

   A. a long beach
   B. a golf course
   C. a mountain range
   D. a tobacco field

3. Where were the first shots of the Civil War fired?

   _____

4. In the sentence,
   "South Carolina wasn't always a golfer's paradise,"
   the word *paradise* means _____.

   A. beach
   B. finding your way
   C. golf course
   D. place of happiness

5. South Carolina's rice industry collapsed after the Civil War. This was due to several reasons. Can you think of one reason why the rice industry in this state did not survive?

   _____

   _____

   _____

   _____

   _____

SOUTH CAROLINA

SOUTH DAKOTA

State Facts

Nickname: _____

Became a State: _____

State Bird: _____

State Flower: _____

State Tree: _____

Fun Fact: _____

What do George Washington, Thomas Jefferson, Abraham Lincoln, and Theodore Roosevelt have in common? They were all great American presidents, but there's another connection. The faces of these men are all carved into the side of South Dakota's Mount Rushmore.

Mount Rushmore is part of a small mountain range called the Black Hills. Looking out from these hills, it's hard to believe that most of South Dakota is farmland. Thick forests cover the Black Hills. Streams topple over granite cliffs. Gold mines lie beneath your feet. The barren Badlands are nearby. Tourists, and towns supporting tourism, are more common there than farms.

The rest of South Dakota is a blanket of ranches and pastures. The Missouri River runs south through the middle of the state, dividing the prairie into east and west. Cattle and sheep graze in green meadows. Fields of corn, soybeans, and wheat wave in the prairie wind. These fertile plains were once grassland. The Arikara Indians farmed; the Cheyenne and Sioux tribes hunted buffalo. The first white settlers were only interested in furs. The Missouri River became their fur-trading highway. Pierre, the state capital, was built along the banks of this river.

The discovery of gold in the Black Hills changed life in South Dakota. A previous treaty with the Sioux Indians had created the Great Sioux Reservation, which included the Black Hills. When prospectors flooded the Black Hills area, the Sioux were forced to give up their land. Crazy Horse, a Sioux Indian chief, resisted this move. A sculpture of Crazy Horse is being carved into the hillside to honor the nation's Native Americans. Today, South Dakota has one of the largest Native American populations in the country. Most live on reservations throughout the state.

Crazy Horse, Washington, Jefferson, Lincoln, and Roosevelt were each great in his own way. These five men lived over a span of nearly two centuries. In South Dakota, they will stand together for centuries to come.

Historical South Dakota

A time line and a list of important events in South Dakota's history are shown below. Each event is labeled with a letter. Use an encyclopedia or another resource to research these events. List these events in *chronological order* (in order of occurrence) on the time line by filling in each box with the appropriate event letter. The letters, in order, will tell how Mount Rushmore was carved.

M Gold was discovered in the Black Hills.

I North and South Dakota were both declared states on the same day. President Benjamin Harrison shuffled the declaration papers before signing, so no one really knows which paper was signed first. North Dakota is considered the 39th state and South Dakota is considered the 40th—since *N* comes before *S* in the alphabet!

T Sculptor Gutzon Borglum started working on the Mount Rushmore National Memorial.

E Sculptor Korczak Ziolkowski started working on the Crazy Horse Memorial.

N The Dakota Territory was established. It included present-day South and North Dakota, Montana, and Wyoming.

D The LaVerendrye brothers claimed South Dakota for France.

A The United States government signed the Laramie Treaty with South Dakota's Sioux Indians.

Y The United States purchased the South Dakota area from France as part of the Louisiana Purchase.

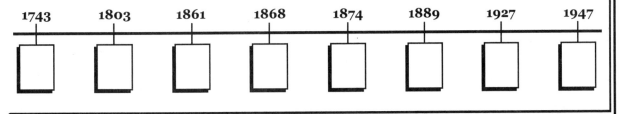

1743	1803	1861	1868	1874	1889	1927	1947

Comprehension Questions

1. The faces of five American presidents are carved into the side of Mount Rushmore.

   True or false? _____

2. Crazy Horse was a member of which Native American tribe?

   A. Arikara
   B. Cherokee
   C. Cheyenne
   D. Sioux

3. Name three crops that are grown in South Dakota.

   _____   _____

   _____

4. In the sentence,
   "When prospectors flooded the Black Hills area, the Sioux were forced to give up their land,"
   the word *flooded* means _____.

   A. boated through
   B. filled
   C. river
   D. watered

5. The faces of George Washington, Thomas Jefferson, Abraham Lincoln, and Theodore Roosevelt are carved into Mount Rushmore. Give one reason why each president was chosen for this national memorial.

   _____

   _____

   _____

   _____

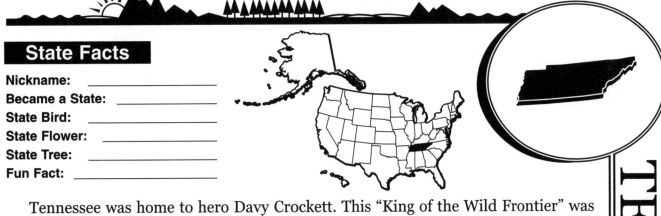

State Facts

Nickname: _____
Became a State: _____
State Bird: _____
State Flower: _____
State Tree: _____
Fun Fact: _____

TENNESSEE

Tennessee was home to hero Davy Crockett. This "King of the Wild Frontier" was famous for his exaggerated tall tales. If Crockett were alive today, what Tennessee Tall Tales would he be telling?

Maybe he would say, "Tennessee is the most neighborly state in the country." According to a map, this tall tale is actually true. Tennessee and Missouri share the prize for bordering the most states. Each has eight state "neighbors."

He could also tell the tale that, "Without Tennessee, there wouldn't be American music." This tall tale has something to do with Tennessee's rich musical history. Nashville, the state capital, is the country music capital of the nation. Tennessee's largest city, Memphis, is the "Birthplace of the Blues." Memphis was also home to Elvis Presley, the "King of Rock and Roll."

Davy Crockett might claim that, "Tennessee stayed with the Union during the Civil War." Now that's a tall tale! Tennessee *seceded* (broke away) from the Union with the other southern Confederate States. However, Tennessee was the very last state to leave the Union at the start of the war, and the very first to return after the end of the war. More Civil War battles were fought on Tennessee soil than anywhere else, except Virginia.

Perhaps Davy Crockett would say, "There are so many mountains in Tennessee that even the rivers get lost!" This tall tale must be referring to the Tennessee River. This river runs through eastern Tennessee. It winds its way in and out of the Blue Ridge Mountains before heading south out of the state. Then, it gets "lost" in Alabama. Eventually it finds its way back into western Tennessee, flowing north all the way to Kentucky. The big bend in this river is the reason why Tennessee is sometimes called the "Big Bend State." There are no mountains in western Tennessee. The fertile land close to the Mississippi River is suited for farmers raising cotton and tobacco.

"Tennessee is a state of farmers." Not anymore, Mr. Crockett. Farmland covers half the state, but more people live in cities than on farms. They work in businesses and factories. They produce chemicals and cars. And right now, some new Tennessee heroes are probably spinning their own tall tales.

Measuring Tennessee's Borders

Most American states border a few other states, but Tennessee and Missouri border each border eight states—more than any other state! The graph below shows all of Tennessee's neighbors, as well as the length of the border that each of these states shares with Tennessee. The border direction (north, south, east, or west) for each of these neighboring states is indicated in brackets beside its name.

Use the graph below to answer the following questions about Tennessee's borders. All numbers are approximate.

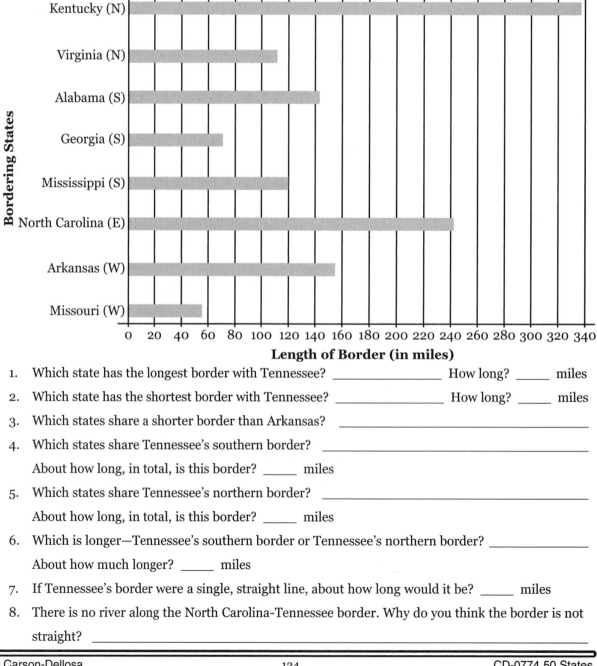

1. Which state has the longest border with Tennessee? _____ How long? _____ miles

2. Which state has the shortest border with Tennessee? _____ How long? _____ miles

3. Which states share a shorter border than Arkansas? _____

4. Which states share Tennessee's southern border? _____
   About how long, in total, is this border? _____ miles

5. Which states share Tennessee's northern border? _____
   About how long, in total, is this border? _____ miles

6. Which is longer—Tennessee's southern border or Tennessee's northern border? _____
   About how much longer? _____ miles

7. If Tennessee's border were a single, straight line, about how long would it be? _____ miles

8. There is no river along the North Carolina-Tennessee border. Why do you think the border is not straight? _____

Comprehension Questions

1. During the Civil War, Tennessee fought on the side of the Union.

   True or false? _____

2. Which of the following statements concerning the city of Memphis is NOT true?

   A. Memphis is called the "Birthplace of the Blues."
   B. Memphis is the capital of Tennessee.
   C. Memphis is the largest city in Tennessee.
   D. Memphis was home to Elvis Presley.

3. What important crops are grown in Tennessee?

   _____   _____

4. In the sentence,
   "The fertile land close to the Mississippi River is suited for farmers raising cotton and tobacco,"
   the word *suited* means _____.

   A. frontier
   B. irrigated
   C. dressed for
   D. right for

5. A tall tale is an exaggerated story. Most tall tales are based on facts. Write down a fact about yourself. Then, write a one-sentence tall tale based on that fact.

   _____

   _____

   _____

   _____

   _____

TEXAS

State Facts

Nickname: _____

Became a State: _____

State Bird: _____

State Flower: _____

State Tree: _____

Fun Fact: _____

Texas is called the Lone Star State. For three centuries, Spanish explorers and missionaries were the only Europeans interested in Texas. The Caddo Indians and other tribes had little contact with Americans to the east. When Mexico broke away from Spain in 1821, Texas became part of Mexico. Under Stephen Austin's leadership, the first of many American settlers moved into the Texas area of Mexico. By 1835, these *Anglos* (non-Spanish-speaking whites) were ready for their own independence. Sam Houston led the Anglo settlers to victory against Mexico in the Texas Revolution.

For nine years after gaining independence from Mexico, Texas was the lone star of a separate country named The Republic of Texas. In 1845, the United States took over this republic. Texas's single star was added to the 27 existing stars on the flag of the United States of America. Texas was now the 28th state.

Texas is huge; only Alaska is bigger. The "Lone Star State" stretches almost 800 miles across the southern part of the country. Most of this vast, dry land is rolling plains, ideal for grazing cattle and growing cotton. The Texas Panhandle is a rectangular piece of land that juts north between Oklahoma and New Mexico. This is where much of the state's plentiful oil is found. The warm waters of the Gulf of Mexico wash up against coastal sand bars. Ships travel in and out of Texas's many ocean ports. Mexico lies to the south, separated from Texas by the waters of the Rio Grande.

Texas is a diverse state in which to live and work. There are many Texan cowhands, decked out in cowboy boots and ten-gallon hats. Texas also has oil workers wearing hard-hats, scientists sporting lab coats, and astronauts in spacesuits. Houston is the center for NASA's manned spacecraft projects.

The word *Texas* comes from a Caddo word for "friends." The state motto is "friendship." There are a lot of friends to make in Texas. Texas has a higher population than any state except California. Texas may be the "Lone Star State," but it's hard to be lonesome with all those people!

Who Am I?

Texas is the second most populous state in the country. There are over 20 million people living in Texas today. Many Texans have played a role in the history of their state, and of the country.

Below is a list of clues. Each clue is associated with a Texan. Each Texan's name is listed in a star. Use an encyclopedia or another resource to help uncover the identities of these Texan riddlers.

1. "I was commander of the victorious Allied forces during the second World War. Later, I became the 34th president of the United States. My friends called me Ike.
   Who am I?" _____

2. "I was a top female athlete. I won gold medals in javelin and hurdles at the 1932 Los Angeles Summer Olympic Games. I followed that up with numerous victories as a professional golfer.
   Who am I?" _____

3. "I was Vice President of the United States under President John F. Kennedy. I became the 36th president after the assassination of Kennedy in Dallas, Texas.
   Who am I?" _____

4. "I was a young rock-and-roller from Lubbock, Texas. My band was called the Crickets, and our biggest hit was 'That'll Be The Day.' I was killed in a plane crash in 1959, at the age of 22.
   Who am I?" _____

5. "I was Vice President of the United States during Franklin Roosevelt's first two terms in office (1933-1941). Folks called me 'Cactus Jack.' "
   Who am I?" _____

6. "I was a World War II hero. I received 28 medals (including the Medal of Honor) from three different countries. I was only 21 by the time the war ended. After I returned home, I became a movie star.
   Who am I?" _____

7. "I was born in Brownsville in 1824, when Texas was still part of Mexico. After the Mexican War, I fought for the rights of Mexican Americans in Texas. My followers called me the 'Robin Hood of South Texas.' I became governor of the Mexican state of Tamaulipas in 1869.
   Who am I?" _____

TEXAS

Juan Cortina

Mildred "Babe" Didrikson Zaharias

Dwight Eisenhower

John Garner

Buddy Holly

Lyndon Johnson

Audie Murphy

TEXAS

Comprehension Questions

1. In 1840, Texas was an independent republic.

   True or false? _____

2. Where is the Texas Panhandle located?

   A. between Arkansas and Oklahoma
   B. between Mexico and the Gulf of Mexico
   C. between New Mexico and Mexico
   D. between New Mexico and Oklahoma

3. What is the most important mineral resource found in Texas?

   _____

4. In the sentence,
   "Texas also has oil workers wearing hard-hats, scientists sporting lab coats, and astronauts in spacesuits,"
   the word *sporting* means _____.

   A. athlete
   B. hiding
   C. running
   D. wearing

5. Houston is the largest city in Texas. Austin is the capital of Texas. Where do you think these cities got their names?

   _____

   _____

   _____

   _____

   _____

Nickname: _____

Became a State: _____

State Bird: _____

State Flower: _____

State Tree: _____

Fun Fact: _____

UTAH

When Brigham Young reached Utah in 1847, he told his followers, "This is the place." Young was the leader of a religious group called the Church of Jesus Christ of Latter-Day Saints. The Latter-Day Saints (sometimes referred to as Mormons) had already been driven out of several states. Their promised land was a barren desert that only native Ute and Navajo tribes wanted. The industrious settlers quickly got to work. Within a few years they had established towns and irrigation systems. They transformed parts of the dry desert into farmland for cattle and cotton. Today, Salt Lake City serves as the Latter-Day Saint Church world headquarters.

Salt Lake City is the state capital and the largest city in Utah. It is located in northern Utah, just south of the Great Salt Lake. Mineral-filled river water flows into this lake, but nothing flows out. The freshwater evaporates, leaving salt behind. It's hard to drown in the Great Salt Lake. The extra salt increases a swimmer's buoyancy; this allows a swimmer to float easily.

West of the Great Salt Lake is one of Utah's three deserts. Parts of this desert are covered in dried salt. Race cars zoom around a speedway that has been built on these flat salt beds. Two ranges of the Rockies run through Utah: the Wasatch Mountains run down the center of the state, and the Uinta Mountains run across the state from Colorado to Salt Lake City. These mountains have turned Utah into a skier's paradise.

Salt isn't the only mineral Utah has to offer. Oil, natural gas, coal, copper, gold, silver—you name it, Utah's got it. But perhaps the most important natural resource in Utah is the earth itself. Wind and water have *eroded* (broken down) the soft sandstone into fantastic shapes. Iron and manganese metals have colored the rock spectacular shades of red, yellow, and purple. The Navajo and Ute Indians have considered some of these rock formations sacred for centuries. Visitors can admire nature's masterpieces in Utah's many national parks.

Pass the Salt, Please!

UTAH

The Great Salt Lake was once part of an ancient freshwater lake called Lake Bonneville. When the waters of Lake Bonneville evaporated, salt, and other minerals were left behind in large sink holes. The Great Salt Lake was formed from one of these holes.

The Great Salt Lake is a terminal lake—fresh water flows from several rivers into the lake, but nothing flows out. This leaves the Great Salt Lake at the mercy of the weather. The water level rises during heavy rains, and falls during periods of drought. As it shrinks, the lake contains a higher percentage of salt. In 1957-59, a *causeway* (raised railway path) was built across the Great Salt Lake, separating the lake into two sections. These sections are called the North and South Arms. Use the graph below to answer the questions about the *salinity* (percentage of salt) of the Great Salt Lake.

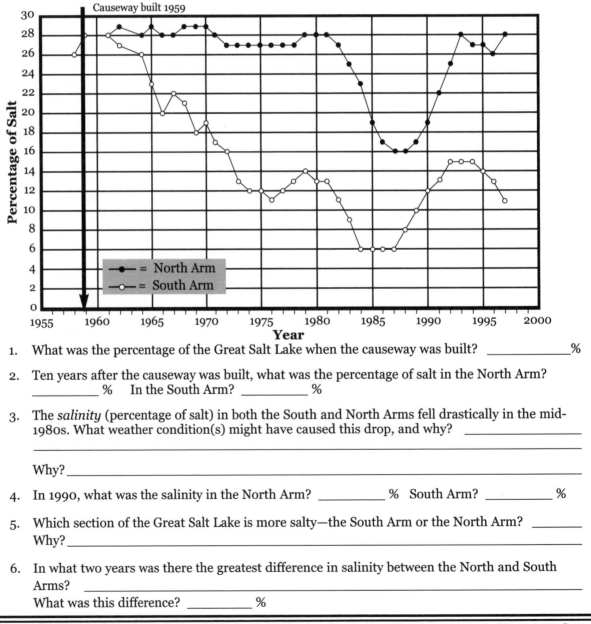

1. What was the percentage of the Great Salt Lake when the causeway was built? _____%

2. Ten years after the causeway was built, what was the percentage of salt in the North Arm? _____ %   In the South Arm? _____ %

3. The *salinity* (percentage of salt) in both the South and North Arms fell drastically in the mid-1980s. What weather condition(s) might have caused this drop, and why? _____
   _____

   Why? _____

4. In 1990, what was the salinity in the North Arm? _____ %   South Arm? _____ %

5. Which section of the Great Salt Lake is more salty—the South Arm or the North Arm? _____
   Why? _____

6. In what two years was there the greatest difference in salinity between the North and South Arms? _____
   What was this difference? _____ %

Comprehension Questions

1. Deserts cover most of the state of Utah.

   True or false? _____

2. Which of the following statements is false?

   A. The Great Salt Lake is located in southern Utah.
   B. Navajo Indian tribes live in Utah.
   C. Salt Lake City is the capital of Utah.
   D. Utah was first settled by Mormons.

3. Name two mountain ranges that are found in Utah.

   _____   _____

4. In the sentence,
   "The industrious settlers quickly got to work,"
   the word *industrious* means _____.

   A. hard-working
   B. mainly manufacturing
   C. newly arrived
   D. religious

5. Rainbow Bridge is one of the seven natural wonders of the world. It is located on the Navajo Reservation in Utah's Monument Valley. Rainbow Bridge is made from sandstone that has been eroded by water and wind. Considering the name of this natural wonder, what do you think this stone formation looks like? Draw a picture of this "bridge" in the box to the right.

VERMONT

State Facts

Nickname: _____
Became a State: _____
State Bird: _____
State Flower: _____
State Tree: _____
Fun Fact: _____

For years, Vermont was caught in the middle of several real-life games of tug-of-war. Before Europeans arrived, this war was between Algonquian and Iroquois tribes. In 1609, Samuel de Champlain discovered Lake Champlain. Champlain claimed the entire Vermont area for France, including the tree-covered Green Mountains. Then, Britain came on the scene. The fight between these two countries ended with British victory in 1763.

By then, another "war" had started. This time it was between the New Hampshire and New York colonies. Once again, Vermont was in the middle. First, the Vermont area was considered part of the New Hampshire colony. Several years later, the border separating the New Hampshire and New York colonies was moved to the Connecticut River. This left the Vermont area as part of the New York colony. New York started giving away Vermont land grants as well. Ethan Allen and the Green Mountain Boys (soldiers already settled in the Vermont area) fought to drive out the New York settlers. This battle only ended with the start of the American Revolution. Settlers from all colonies forgot their squabbles and united to defeat the British.

After the Revolutionary War, Vermont insisted upon being an independent republic—separate from both New York and New Hampshire. In 1791, Vermont finally won its long game of tug-of-war. The "Green Mountain State" became the first state to join the Union after the original Thirteen Colonies.

Although Vermont doesn't touch the ocean, it's still part of New England. Mining produces granite, marble, and slate. Industry and manufacturing are important. However, unlike Vermont's neighbors, Vermont remains very rural. Only one-third of its small population lives in cities. Its largest city, Burlington, has a population of only 40,000. Montpelier is the least populated state capital in the country, with a population of 8,000.

Vermont's quiet towns, small dairy farms, and beautiful mountains (Green, White, and Taconic ranges) attract tourists. Autumn paints the forested hills in brilliant colors. Skiers enjoy heavy winter snow. Visitors snack on sweet maple syrup in the spring, and hikers tramp along wooded trails in the cool summer.

Sugaring in Vermont

Vermont is the country's largest producer of maple syrup. It takes about 40 gallons of sugar maple sap to produce a single gallon of maple syrup. Vermont's climate is perfect for sugaring. The sap starts flowing in late winter and early spring. Sugarmakers drill holes in the trees and attach taps, or spouts. The sap drips into hanging buckets, which are then collected, and the sap is poured into a storage tank. The sugarmaker carefully boils the sap to remove the extra water. Maple syrup is eaten plain, on pancakes or waffles. It's also used to make maple butter, fudge, jelly, and other delicious foods. Sugar-on-snow is a taffy-like candy made from maple syrup. Just drizzle boiled syrup onto cold, clean snow and—presto!—you've got sugar-on-snow.

Imagine that three people from three different places are visiting Vermont. Each visitor is touring a different sugarhouse and purchasing a different maple sugar product. Each sugarhouse will only sell one type of product to each of these customers. Match the visitors with their homes, sugarhouses visited, and maple sugar purchases. First, read the clues. If something cannot be true, put an X in that box. If something is true, put a ✓ in that box, and then put X's in the other two boxes in that row and column. Study the ✓s and X's in the chart to uncover more information, filling in more as you go. If two of the boxes in a row or column already have X's in them, then put a ✓ in the third box. You may have to read the clues more than once. Use a map of Vermont to help you.

Clues
1. The visitor from the Canadian province did not bring home any fudge or syrup.
2. One of the tourists traveled just 20 miles west of her hometown, crossing the Connecticut River to reach a sugarhouse in nearby St. Johnsbury.
3. The sugarhouse closest to Lake Champlain was only selling sugar-on-snow.
4. The New Yorker traveled to the southernmost Vermont sugarhouse.
5. The visitor from the neighboring New England state did not buy maple syrup.

		Location of Sugarhouse			Maple Product Purchased		
		Brattleboro	St. Albans	St. Johnsbury	Maple fudge	Maple syrup	Sugar-on-snow
Visitor's home state or province	New York						
	New Hampshire						
	Quebec						
Maple Products Sold	Maple fudge						
	Maple syrup						
	Sugar-on-snow						

Comprehension Questions

1. Vermont is considered the 14th state.

   True or false? _____

2. Who were the Green Mountain Boys?

   A. British spies
   B. farmers from New York
   C. French explorers
   D. soldiers from the Vermont area

3. Name three of Vermont's most important non-metallic minerals.

   _____   _____

   _____

4. In the sentence,
   "However, unlike Vermont's neighbors, Vermont remains very rural,"
   the word *rural* means _____.

   A. people living in the city
   B. people living in the country
   C. rough
   D. small

5. The United States Census is a survey that is done every decade. This survey counts the number of people living in the United States that year. According to the 2000 census, there are about 600,000 people who live in Vermont. One-third of these people live in cities or towns. Approximately how many people live in the country— that is, not in a city or town? Burlington is Vermont's largest city. It has a population of approximately 40,000 people. Approximately how many people live in Vermont's cities or towns, NOT including Burlington? Show your work.

   _____

   _____

   _____

State Facts

Nickname: _____

Became a State: _____

State Bird: _____

State Flower: _____

State Tree: _____

Fun Fact: _____

When Spanish missionaries settled on Virginia's shores in the mid-1500s, the Spaniards did not last long. The Powhatan Indians quickly wiped out the Spanish settlement. Thirty-seven years later, English settlers sailed up the James River. These treasure-seekers settled in Jamestown, in the middle of Powhatan territory. Luckily for the settlers, the Indians held back. Jamestown became the country's first permanent European settlement.

At first, it seemed as if starvation would kill off the newcomers. But within five years, they had adapted to their new world. They planted corn and tobacco. They concentrated on survival and forgot about gold. John Smith, their leader, made peace with Chief Powhatan. Powhatan's daughter, Pocahontas, even married a tobacco planter. By the time the Powhatan Tribe rebelled against the settlers, it was too late. The settlers were there to stay.

By 1775, the American colonists had decided to break away from England. The Continental Congress met in Williamsburg in 1776. George Washington, a Virginia planter, was elected as the army's commander-in-chief. Many Revolutionary War battles were fought in Virginia, including the 1781 British surrender at Yorktown, Virginia.

Virginia has given the country many famous politicians. Four of the first five presidents, as well as four later presidents, were born here. Confederate General Robert E. Lee was also a Virginian. The Civil War ended at Appomattox, Virginia, when Lee was forced to surrender to Union forces.

The Blue Ridge Mountains have separated West Virginia from Virginia since the Civil War. Chesapeake Bay is to the east. Virginia's coastline is a maze of rivers and inlets. The Delmarva Peninsula's southern tip is part of Virginia, too. Virginia has many summer resorts and sandy beaches.

Virginia's economy is diversified—it doesn't rely on just one industry. Tobacco is important (particularly for Richmond, the capital), but so are turkeys. Factories make synthetic fibers and roll out transportation equipment. Shipyards build ships. Coal miners dig coal. Fishing fleets bring in crabs and oysters. Tourists line up to see historic attractions, as well as beautiful scenery. The federal government in nearby Washington, D.C., provides jobs for many Virginians.

Virginian Ups and Downs

Use an atlas, encyclopedia, or other resource to help you complete this crossword puzzle.

Across

1. At the start of the American Revolution, Virginian patriot Patrick Henry said, "Give me _ _ _ _ _ _ _ or give me death!"
5. The name of Thomas Jefferson's home
7. Virginia, to the post office
9. Virginia is a big producer of this type of meat.
11. On a map, Virginia looks roughly like this geometric shape.
12. The name of a river, valley, mountain range and National Park found in northwestern Virginia.

Down

2. The number of Presidents born in Virginia
3. The last name of the 28th President
4. Virginia's nickname: "Old _ _ _ _ _ _ _ _"
5. The last name of the 4th President
6. In the southeastern corner of Virginia, the Dismal Swamp runs into _ _ _ _ _ Carolina.
8. Mount _ _ _ _ _ _ is George Washington's home.
10. This bay separates the Delmarva Peninsula from the rest of Virginia.
12. John _ _ _ _ _ , early Jamestown colonist

The first permanent American settlers sailed across the Atlantic Ocean in three ships. What were the names of these three Virginian ships? Use the first letters of your clue answers to find out.

__ U __ A __   __ O __ __ __ A __ __ ,   G O __ __ P __ __ __ ,
12D 12D 6D   10D   6D 12A 11A 6D 11A   4D 12A 2D 2D 4D

and __ I __ __ O V __ R Y
      4D 12D 10D   2D

Comprehension Questions

1. Nine presidents of the United States were born in Virginia.

   True or false? _____

2. Where did the last battle of the Civil War take place?

   A. Appomattox, Virginia
   B. Jamestown, Virginia
   C. Williamsburg, Virginia
   D. Yorktown, Virginia

3. What is the capital of Virginia?

   _____

4. In the sentence,
   "The Powhatan Indians quickly wiped out the Spanish settlement,"
   the phrase *wiped out* means _____.

   A. cleaned
   B. ignored
   C. killed
   D. moved

5. Virginia's economy is diversified. What does the word *diversified* mean? Why is it good to have a diversified economy?

   _____

   _____

   _____

   _____

   _____

   _____

State Facts

Nickname: _____

Became a State: _____

State Bird: _____

State Flower: _____

State Tree: _____

Fun Fact: _____

You're standing in a jungle of tall fir trees. Green moss covers the trunks. You know glacier-topped mountains are close by, but you're stuck in a forest of ferns. You hear ocean waves beating against the rocky coast, but you can't see the water. You can't even see the sky—the leaves are too thick! Where are you? You're on the Olympic Peninsula, in northwestern Washington. And you might be very wet! Here in the Olympic Peninsula, irrigation isn't required. Up to 12 feet of rain falls every year.

The Olympic Peninsula is a small part of the state of Washington, but it's the least affected by modern life. Native American tribes such as the Makah and Quinault live along the ocean coast, but most of this peninsula remains wilderness. Washington borders the Pacific Ocean. The ocean brings rain. In some areas, you can go weeks without seeing the sun.

The Strait of Juan de Fuca connects the Pacific with Puget Sound. Most of Washington's cities—including Seattle (the largest) and Olympia (the capital), are located near this water. Ships traveling to Alaska and Asia dock in Puget Sound's many protected harbors. Cities here started as ports for shipping Washington's plentiful lumber. Now, these cities are centers of business (Microsoft, Boeing, and other high-tech firms) and trade. Salmon fishing remains important. Cities further inland specialize in farming, logging, or mining. Washington has several large Indian reservations, including reservations for the Colville and Yakama tribes.

The Olympic Mountains aren't the state's only high points. Washington's four corners are topped with mountains. The biggest of all Washington's hills is the volcanic Cascade Range in the center of the state. Glaciers are common in the high peaks, and winter snow is heavy. In 1980, Mount St. Helens erupted. Fifty-seven people were killed, and the surrounding land was covered with ash.

Eastern Washington is much drier than western Washington. But even in the driest areas, farmers grow record wheat crops. Water from the state's many rivers, including the Columbia and Snake, helps with irrigation.

Piecing Together Washington's Flora and Fauna

The state of Washington is the 18th largest state in the country, and the smallest of all western states. Within this state you will find towering mountains, ocean coasts, raging rivers, and inland plains. All this diversity in land means that Washington can support many kinds of *flora* (plant life) and *fauna* (animal life).

Below are two lists. Each word from List A belongs with a word from List B. Together, these words make up a two-word name of a plant or animal found in Washington. Use a dictionary, encyclopedia, or another resource to piece together these names. Write the correct word from List A in the spaces in front of the corresponding word from List B.

(Hints: Treat the boxed letters just like a space. Don't worry if there are more spaces than you need. Check off the List A words as you go along. The first two-word name has been done for you.)

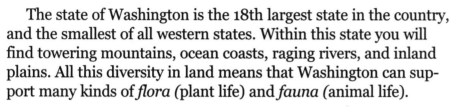

List A		List B
____BANANA	S E A _ _ _ _ _ _ _	OTTER
____DOUGLAS	_ _ _ _ _ ☐ _ _ _	ELK
____GRIZZLY	_ _ _ _ _ _ ☐ _	FERN
____JUMPING	_ _ _ _ ☐ _ _ _	PINE
____KILLER	_ _ _ ☐ _ _ _ _	FIR
____LICORICE	_ ☐ _ _ _ ☐ _ _	BEAR
____MOUNTAIN	_ _ _ ☐ _ _ _ _	TROUT
____PONDEROSA	_ _ _ _ ☐ _ _ _	SALMON
____ROOSEVELT	_ _ _ _ ☐ _ _ _	MOUSE
____SEA	☐ _ _ _ _ _ _ _	OWL
____SITKA	_ _ _ _ ☐ _ _ _	CARIBOU
____SOCKEYE	_ _ _ ☐ _ _ _ _	SLUG
____SPOTTED	_ _ ☐ _ _ _ _ _	SPRUCE
____STEELHEAD	_ _ _ _ ☐ _ _ _	WHALE

When you have completed piecing together the names of these flora and fauna species, the boxed letters, in order, will spell out the popular nickname of this western state.

__ __ __ __ __ __ __ __ __ __ __ __ __ __ __

Comprehension Questions

1. Seattle is the capital of Washington.

   True or false? _____

2. Which of the following Native American tribes does NOT live in Washington?

   A. Colville
   B. Lenape
   C. Makah
   D. Yakama

3. What type of fish is important to Washington's economy?

   _____

4. In the sentence,
   "But even in the driest areas, farmers grow record wheat crops,"
   the word *record* means _____.

   A. CDs of
   B. great amounts of
   C. musical
   D. written statistics

5. Seattle and other cities in Puget Sound play an important role in trade with Asian countries. Why?

   _____

   _____

   _____

   _____

   _____

   _____

WASHINGTON

State Facts

Nickname: _____
Became a State: _____
State Bird: _____
State Flower: _____
State Tree: _____
Fun Fact: _____

WEST VIRGINIA

West Virginia was created on June 20, 1863, during the Civil War. The state of Virginia had already *seceded* (withdrawn) from the Union. Actually, most people living in Virginia's western counties wanted to stay within the Union. So they stayed. They separated from Virginia and created a brand new state. The new state was made up of land west of the Allegheny Mountains, plus a few counties along the Potomac River in the north.

West Virginia was in a tough position between northern (Union) states and southern (Confederate) states. Hundreds of battles were fought within its borders. Towns, even families, were split between the two sides. Victory for the Union eventually united the nation, but the states remained separate. Today, June 20th is still celebrated in the "Mountain State" as West Virginia Day.

Even before 1863, the Appalachians were a natural barrier between the two states. West Virginia's forested mountains were created thousands of years ago from folded layers of rock. These rock layers formed the steep Allegheny Mountains in the east. The Appalachian Plateau, with more ridges and valleys, covers the rest of the state. The mountains are highest in the east, sloping down toward the Ohio River. Rivers run along most of West Virginia's uneven borders. The mountainous interior is filled with streams and waterfalls. Heavy rains and flash flooding are regular hazards.

West Virginia has few large cities. The capital, Charleston, is the largest. Apples and peaches are grown in the eastern panhandle between Maryland and Virginia. Livestock, mainly poultry and cattle, are raised in river valleys. Apart from the scenery, Mother Nature's treasures lie beneath the mountain forests: natural gas, oil, and coal—lots and lots of coal! For the past 100 years, coal has shaped the state's economy. European immigrants flocked to the coal mines. Miners battled owners for better working conditions. Today, environmentalists still push for a cleaner coal industry.

W..E..S..T....V..I..R..G..I..N..I..A

Learn more about the state of West Virginia. Use a dictionary, encyclopedia, or atlas to help you fill in the blanks in the sentences below. Each of the missing words starts with the corresponding letter in the name West Virginia.

W — Between 1863 and 1870, and again between 1875 and 1885, the state capital was located at W __ __ __ __ __ __ __, in the narrow northern panhandle between Ohio and Pennsylvania.

E — Charleston lies at the junction of two rivers: the Kanawha and the E __ __.

S — West Virginia is famous for its enormous deposits of *bituminous* (s __ __ __) coal. Very little of the coal found in the Appalachians is *anthracite* (hard coal).

T — Confederate General T __ __ __ __ __ (Stonewall) Jackson was born in Clarksburg in 1824. His troops nicknamed him Stonewall because he held the enemy back like a "stone wall."

V — Even before the American Revolution, a proposal was made to separate West Virginia from Virginia. This 14th colony was to be called V __ __ __ __ __ __ __. Today, that name is given to a tiny village located east of Stonewall Jackson Lake in central West Virginia.

I — In 1859, John Brown (under the name I __ __ __ __ Smith) moved to Harper's Ferry. He later robbed a federal armory in an attempt to arm his anti-slavery gang. Brown was hanged as a traitor, but his name became associated with anti-slavery beliefs.

R — The town of R __ __ __ __ __ on the South Branch Potomac River was taken over by both Union and Confederate troops at least 50 different times during the Civil War.

G — The Adena Indians were mound-builders—prehistoric people who created monuments for their dead out of dirt and stone. The G __ __ __ __ Creek Mound near Moundsville is one of the tallest of these monuments.

I — In 1807, former vice-president Aaron Burr and supporter Harmon Blennerhassett were arrested for *treason* (betraying their country). Blennerhassett's mansion can still be seen at Blennerhassett I __ __ __ __ __ Historical State Park on the Ohio River near Parkersburg.

N — The N __ __ River, in the southern part of the state, is actually one of the oldest rivers in North America. It was part of an ancient river system called the Teays.

I — Industrial cities along the Ohio River manufacture huge quantities of steel and i __ __ __.

A — Nancy Hanks was born on a farm near Keyser, on the North Branch Potomac River close to the Maryland border. She grew up to become the mother of "Honest A__ __ Lincoln."

Comprehension Questions

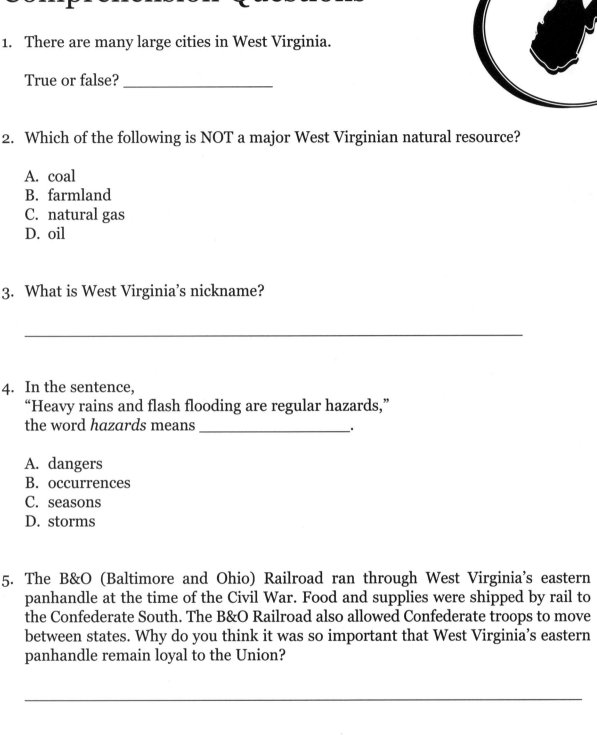

1. There are many large cities in West Virginia.

    True or false? _____

2. Which of the following is NOT a major West Virginian natural resource?

    A. coal
    B. farmland
    C. natural gas
    D. oil

3. What is West Virginia's nickname?

    _____

4. In the sentence,
    "Heavy rains and flash flooding are regular hazards,"
    the word *hazards* means _____.

    A. dangers
    B. occurrences
    C. seasons
    D. storms

5. The B&O (Baltimore and Ohio) Railroad ran through West Virginia's eastern panhandle at the time of the Civil War. Food and supplies were shipped by rail to the Confederate South. The B&O Railroad also allowed Confederate troops to move between states. Why do you think it was so important that West Virginia's eastern panhandle remain loyal to the Union?

    _____

    _____

    _____

    _____

State Facts

Nickname: _____
Became a State: _____
State Bird: _____
State Flower: _____
State Tree: _____
Fun Fact: _____

When Madison was chosen as the capital of the Wisconsin Territory in 1836, it was only a sketch on paper. Madison was in the middle of nowhere. Its neighbors were lakes, trees, and furry mammals which kept the fur trade booming. Today, a major cross-country highway passes through Madison. Wisconsin's capital is home to over 200,000 people.

Wisconsin borders the shores of two of the Great Lakes (Lake Michigan and Lake Superior). The St. Croix and Mississippi Rivers lie to the west. These water routes were perfect for the fur trade. Water brought traders into the wilderness and fur pelts out. First French, then British, then American fur traders claimed Wisconsin's land. Originally, they traded with the Winnebago and Menominee Tribes. By the mid-1800s, most tribes had been pushed out.

As Wisconsin opened up to the world, the world came to Wisconsin. Eager miners came to dig for lead. Thousands of immigrants from Northern Europe (mainly Germany) rushed to the state. Today, the fur trade has been replaced by manufacturing (machinery and electronics), dairy farming, and paper product production.

Wisconsin is not mountainous. The highest point, Timms Hill in the northern highlands, doesn't even reach 2,000 feet above sea level. Yet, it is certainly not flat. The glaciers that scraped across the state in the last ice age have left their mark. Fertile valleys are mixed with rocky ridges, miles of pine forests, and thousands of blue lakes. Only Wisconsin's southwest escaped the glaciers. This Driftless Region is the most rugged area in the state, with deep *gorges* (canyons) along the Mississippi River. Wisconsin's central plain is crammed with rivers and waterfalls. The best agricultural land is in the east. It is here that Wisconsin's dairy industry thrives.

More Cheese, Please!

Wisconsin is one of the top cheese-producing states in the country. Many varieties of cheese are created here. Below is a Wisconsin Cheese Chart. Use the chart to answer the following questions.

1. Wisconsin produces the most of which of the following cheeses: other American, cheddar, or mozzarella?

   _____

2. Wisconsin produces the least of which of these cheeses?

   _____

3. How much more mozzarella cheese did Wisconsin produce than cheddar cheese?

   _____ % more mozzarella

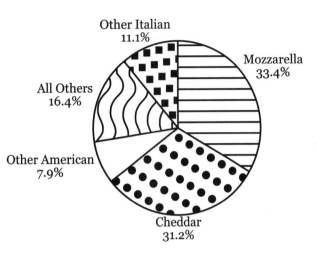

4. How much less other American cheese did Wisconsin produce than all other kinds of cheese combined? _____ %

5. By what percentage did Wisconsin produce more other Italian cheese than other American cheese? _____ % more other Italian

6. Pretend that Wisconsin cheesemakers produce 3.5% Asiago, an Italian cheese. What if Wisconsin dairies decided to make Asiago cheese its own category? How would this affect the percentage of other Italian cheeses? How would the chart look different? Draw and explain your answer below.

_____
_____
_____
_____
_____
_____
_____
_____
_____

WISCONSIN

Comprehension Questions

1. Wisconsin is a mountainous state.

   True or false? _____

2. Which part of Wisconsin was NOT covered by glaciers in the last ice age?

   A. eastern Wisconsin
   B. northwest Wisconsin
   C. southeast Wisconsin
   D. southwest Wisconsin

3. Parts of Wisconsin lie along the shores of which two Great Lakes?

   _____

   _____

4. In the sentence,
   "It is here that Wisconsin's dairy industry thrives,"
   the word *thrives* means _____.

   A. does well
   B. exists
   C. farmland
   D. sits

5. Fur traders of the early centuries relied on water for transporting their goods. Why was water so important for traders in America's wilderness? What about roads?

   _____

   _____

   _____

   _____

State Facts

Nickname: _____

Became a State: _____

State Bird: _____

State Flower: _____

State Tree: _____

Fun Fact: _____

WYOMING

Is there anyone in America who hasn't heard of Yellowstone National Park? Yellowstone is the oldest National Park in the country. It was established in 1872, 18 years before Wyoming even became a state! With its massive mountains, sparkling waterfalls, and plentiful wildlife, it's not hard to see why Yellowstone is Wyoming's greatest tourist attraction.

Then, there are Yellowstone's hot springs! Thousands of years ago, this northwestern corner of Wyoming was an enormous blister of erupting volcanoes. Today, that hot *magma* (molten rock) still lies beneath the Earth's surface. Some of Yellowstone's hot springs reach 400°F—almost 200°F above water's boiling point! In many places, the underground water is under so much pressure that it bursts out of the ground in a sizzling column of water, called a geyser. Old Faithful is the most famous geyser in the world. It erupts so regularly that you can almost set your watch to it.

The federal government owns half of Wyoming's land. South of Yellowstone is Grand Teton National Park. Sprinkled throughout the state are National Forests and Wildlife Preserves. The Rocky Mountains spread southward, making Wyoming one of the highest states in the country. Only Colorado is higher in altitude. The eastern half of Wyoming is part of the Great Plains. The land there is high above sea level, but it's treeless and flat, with plenty of grass for grazing cattle and sheep.

Wyoming's most important natural resource is its land. Tourists come to see, hike, or ski it. Cows like to graze on it, as long as it's covered with grass. And miners like to dig in it. There's more than just magma below Wyoming's surface. There's oil, as well as natural gas, coal, and other minerals.

Fewer people live in Wyoming than in any other state. Many live in small cities and towns. Wyoming's most famous resident was cowboy/showman Buffalo Bill Cody. Cody's traveling Wild West Show brought cowboy life to audiences all over the world. Wyoming will always be remembered as part of the Wild, Wild West.

Jim Bridger's "Lies"

Jim Bridger was an American fur trader, trapper, explorer, and guide. He lived during the 1800s, at a time when more and more pioneers were heading west. Bridger was probably the first white person to see the wonders of Yellowstone National Park. When Bridger told people of the fantastic geysers and bubbling mud pots found in the area, no one believed him. Decades later, when other expeditions finally reached Yellowstone, Jim Bridger's "lies" were discovered to actually be true!

Listed below are 9 sets of Wyoming "truths." Each "truth" is identified with a letter. In each set of "truths," one statement is actually untrue. Use an encyclopedia, atlas or another resource to determine which statements are untrue. Circle them.

1. Interstate highways in Wyoming

   C. I-25
   D. I-76
   E. I-80
   F. I-90

2. National forests in Wyoming

   F. Bridger-Teton National Forest
   G. Medicine Bow National Forest
   H. Shoshone National Forest
   I. Wenatchee National Forest

3. Minerals found in Wyoming

   J. Bentonite
   K. Coal
   L. Silver
   M. Trona

4. Mountain ranges in Wyoming

   M. Bighorn Mountains
   N. Cascade Mountains
   O. Teton Range
   P. Laramie Mountains

5. Historic forts in Wyoming

   M. Fort Henry
   N. Fort Caspar
   O. Fort Bridger
   P. Fort Laramie

6. National wildlife refuges in Wyoming

   A. Columbia National Wildlife Refuge
   B. National Elk Wildlife Refuge
   C. Pathfinder Bird Refuge
   D. Seedskadee National Wildlife Refuge

7. Major geysers in Yellowstone N. P.

   L. Bijou Geyser
   M. Giant Geyser
   N. Old Faithful
   O. Up-She-Goes

8. Major rivers in Wyoming

   S. Bighorn River
   T. Connecticut River
   U. Green River
   V. North Platte River

9. Popular ski areas in Wyoming

   T. Jackson Hole
   U. Pike's Peak
   V. Sleeping Giant
   W. Snow King

10. Mountains in Wyoming

   S. Separation Peak
   T. Hawksbill Mountain
   U. The Thunderer
   V. Pelican Cone

To find out Jim Bridger's nickname, write the Letter Labels of the lies in the blank spaces below.
(Hint: The corresponding Lie # is listed underneath each of the blank spaces.)

   ___ ___ ___ ___ ___ ___ of the ___ ___ ___ ___ ___ ___ ___ ___

LIE # 7 3 1   5 6 4   5 7 9 4 10 6 2 4

WYOMING

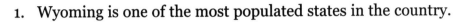

Comprehension Questions

1. Wyoming is one of the most populated states in the country.

    True or false? _____

2. In what part of Wyoming is Yellowstone National Park located?

    A. east
    B. northwest
    C. southeast
    D. southwest

3. In what year did Wyoming become a state?

    _____

4. In the sentence,
    "With its massive mountains, sparkling waterfalls, and plentiful wildlife, it's not
    hard to see why Yellowstone is Wyoming's greatest tourist attraction,"
    the word *plentiful* means _____.

    A. a lot of
    B. scarce
    C. strange
    D. tame

5. A geyser shoots hot water and steam up into the air, similar to the eruption of a
    volcano. The deeper the water lies underground, the higher the eruption. Can you
    think of a reason why?

    _____

    _____

    _____

    _____

    _____

United States Word Search

Find each state name and the District of Columbia in this puzzle (Hint: Refer to page 164 for a list of all fifty states.

```
N A M V M A F D E E Q Q M W E S T V I R G I N I A
O S R O E A L O C J H V J W M I S S I S S I P P I
R O D I N R I A K W Q G K Y R H O D E I S L A N D
T U N I Z T M N C A L I F O R N I A S T P S Q B T
H T E P S O A O E W A S H I N G T O N K J N M C N
C H W E C T N N L O U I S I A N A A Z I K S S U
A C H N O N R A A T N E W M E X I C O H X O Q J O
R A A N N O A I T U J B K D N E W J E R S E Y I B
O R M S N R W P C B N Z O M I S S O U R I F H V G
L O P Y E T A Z T T V G V R O L B I M R P O A N M
I L S L C H I X E A O O E Z E J Q C L W C D I E A
N I H V T D I N N R O F L O U G F O U O A M A M H
A N I A I A E R N K H O C J R D O F J V O N A S C
M A R N C K B Y E A K G V O P G Z N E Y A B T S M
Q I E I U O S Q S N E W R B L T I N W I A T I J A
G L V A T T O M S S N F E H P U O A D L E U B Q R
Y L F O V A U I E A T F Q S H H M N A S I Z O Y Y
C I M K I L T N E S U O D D A I I B U A H O S L L
O N I L R U H N F H C S M D I K A H I K L U W L A
L O C A G M D E V I K Y I A R D C H W A A A T A N
O I H H I U A S G Z Y S W O I A G L I R R N S A D
R S I O N P K O Z G A A Y R S I M D W T P X S K H
A F G M I Z O T H X H W O S N E B R A S K A I A A
D C A A A L T A E L E L A T E S D E L A W A R E S
O I N Y A O A T A N F M W I S C O N S I N L F L O
```

In the top 12 horizontal rows, circle the first unused letter. The unused letters, in order, will complete the sentence below.

__ __ __ __ __ __   and   __ __ __ __ __ __ __

are NOT part of the *contiguous* (sharing a common boundary) United States.

Planting Pie Charts

When Europeans arrived in the United States hundreds of years ago, they learned about corn from their Native American neighbors. Today, more corn is grown in the United States than any other crop. Sorghum is another crop that is grown in the United States. Most of the sorghum grown in this country is fed to livestock. In the United States, we grow almost twenty times more corn than sorghum.

The following pie charts represent the total *annual* (one year) corn and sorghum production in the United States. The four top-producing states for each crop are shown. The remaining states are grouped together in the charts under the label *Other*.

2001 Corn   **2001 Sorghum**

IA   Iowa
IL   Illinois
KS   Kansas
MN   Minnesota
MO   Missouri
NE   Nebraska
TX   Texas

2001 Corn: NE 10%, IA 18%, IL 17%, MN 9%, Other 46%

2001 Sorghum: Other 18%, MO 5%, NE 7%, TX 30%, KS 40%

1. Of the four top-producing corn states, which produced the most corn? _____
    Which produced the least corn? _____

2. Of the four top-producing sorghum states, which produced the most sorghum? _____
    Which produced the least sorghum? _____

3. If all the OTHER states were to stop growing these crops, which crop would be the most affected?
    _____
    Why? _____
    _____
    Which crop would be the least affected? _____
    Why? _____

4. If Minnesota and Nebraska combined their corn production, would they produce more corn than
    Iowa? _____
    If yes, how much more? _____ %

5. If Missouri and Nebraska combined their sorghum production, would they produce more
    sorghum than Kansas? _____
    If yes, how much more? _____ %

6. From looking only at the pie charts, can you tell if Nebraska produced more corn than sorghum?
    Why or why not? _____
    _____

American Borders

The United States borders more water than land. The oceans and countries around its borders have helped shape the culture of the United States. Use a map of the United States to answer the following questions. Write the state abbreviations as your answers.

1. List the states that share a border with Canada: _____

_____

List the states that share a border with Mexico: _____

_____

List the states that share a border with Russia: _____

2. List the states that touch the Arctic Ocean: _____

List the states that touch the the Pacific Ocean: _____

_____

List the states that touch the Atlantic Ocean, including the Gulf of Mexico: _____

_____

_____

Of the states on the Atlantic Ocean, how many border the Gulf of Mexico? _____

3. List the states that touch any of the Great Lakes (Lake Superior, Lake Michigan,

Lake Huron, Lake Erie, Lake Ontario): _____

_____

4. List the states that touch the Mississippi River: _____

_____

5. List the states that share a border with Missouri: _____

_____

List the states that share a border with Massachusetts: _____

List the states that share a border with Mississippi: _____

List the states that share a border with Oregon: _____

List the states that share a border with South Dakota: _____

_____

6. List the states share a border with the nation's capital: _____

UNITED STATES OF AMERICA

Temperature Trends

This chart gives the average summer and winter temperatures for nine of the 50 states. The states are grouped by geographic region: northern, central, and southern. Use the chart to answer the following questions.

	Northern States			Central States			Southern States		
	Washington	Minnesota	Maine	California	Nebraska	Virginia	Arizona	Texas	Florida
Average Temperature in January (Fahrenheit)	30°	08°	15°	44°	23°	36°	41°	46°	59°
Average Temperature in July (Fahrenheit)	66°	70°	67°	75°	76°	75°	80°	83°	81°

1. In January, how much warmer is it in Florida than in Minnesota? _____ ° F

2. In July, how much cooler is it in Maine than in Arizona? _____ ° F

3. In California, how much warmer is it in July than it is in January? _____ ° F

4. In Virginia, how much cooler is it in January than it is in July? _____ ° F

5. Which central state has the coldest January temperature? _____
   Which central state has the warmest July temperature? _____

6. Which state has the warmest average temperature in January? _____
   Which state has the warmest average temperature in July? _____
   What region(s) are these states in? _____

7. Which state has the coolest average temperature in January? _____
   Which state has the coolest average temperature in July? _____
   What region(s) are these states in? _____

8. Which state has the least temperature change between January and July? _____
   What is this temperature change? _____ ° F
   What region is this state in? _____

9. Which state has the greatest temperature change between January and July? _____
   What is this temperature change? _____ ° F
   What region is this state in? _____

10. What conclusions can you draw from the answers to questions 6 and 8, and 7 and 9?

   _____

   _____

   _____

UNITED STATES OF AMERICA

Time Line and State Symbols

The United States declared independence from Britain on July 4, 1776. After the Revolutionary War, the original Thirteen Colonies became the first 13 states. The time line on this page shows when each state joined the Union. Nicknames, flowers, birds, and trees are also shown.

State Name	Became a State	Nickname	State Bird	State Flower	State Tree
Delaware	December 7, 1787	First State	Blue Hen Chicken	Peach Blossom	American Holly
Pennsylvania	December 12, 1787	Keystone State	Ruffed Grouse	Mountain Laurel	Hemlock
New Jersey	December 18, 1787	Garden State	Eastern Goldfinch	Purple Violet	Red Oak
Georgia	January 2, 1788	Peach State	Brown Thrasher	Cherokee Rose	Live Oak
Connecticut	January 9, 1788	Constitution State	American Robin	Mountain Laurel	White Oak
Massachusetts	February 6, 1788	Bay State	Chickadee	Mayflower	American Elm
Maryland	April 28, 1788	Old Line State	Baltimore Oriole	Black-Eyed Susan	White Oak
South Carolina	May 23, 1788	Palmetto State	Carolina Wren	Yellow Jessamine	Palmetto
New Hampshire	June 21, 1788	Granite State	Purple Finch	Purple Lilac	White Birch
Virginia	June 25, 1788	Old Dominion	Cardinal	Dogwood	Dogwood
New York	July 26, 1788	Empire State	Bluebird	Rose	Sugar Maple
North Carolina	November 21, 1789	Tar Heel State	Cardinal	Dogwood	Pine
Rhode Island	May 29, 1790	Ocean State	Rhode Island Red	Violet	Red Maple
Vermont	March 4, 1791	Green Mountain State	Hermit Thrush	Red Clover	Sugar Maple
Kentucky	June 1, 1792	Bluegrass State	Cardinal	Goldenrod	Tulip Poplar
Tennessee	June 1, 1796	Volunteer State	Mockingbird	Iris	Tulip Poplar
Ohio	March 1, 1803	Buckeye State	Cardinal	Scarlet Carnation	Buckeye
Louisiana	April 30, 1812	Pelican State	Eastern Brown Pelican	Magnolia	Cypress
Indiana	December 11, 1816	Hoosier State	Cardinal	Peony	Tulip Poplar
Mississippi	December 10, 1817	Magnolia State	Mockingbird	Magnolia	Magnolia
Illinois	December 3, 1818	Prairie State	Cardinal	Native Violet	White Oak
Alabama	December 14, 1819	Yellowhammer State	Yellowhammer	Camellia	Southern Longleaf Pine
Maine	March 15, 1820	Pine Tree State	Chickadee	White Pine Cone & Tassel	Eastern White Pine
Missouri	August 10, 1821	Show Me State	Bluebird	Hawthorne	Dogwood
Arkansas	June 15, 1836	Natural State	Mockingbird	Apple Blossom	Pine
Michigan	January 26, 1837	Wolverine State	Robin	Apple Blossom	White Pine
Florida	March 3, 1845	Sunshine State	Mockingbird	Orange Blossom	Sabal Palmetto Palm
Texas	December 29, 1845	Lone Star State	Mockingbird	Bluebonnet	Pecan
Iowa	December 28, 1846	Hawkeye State	Eastern Goldfinch	Wild Rose	Oak
Wisconsin	May 29, 1848	Badger State	Robin	Wood Violet	Sugar Maple
California	September 9, 1850	Golden State	California Valley Quail	Golden Poppy	California Redwood
Minnesota	May 11, 1858	North Star State	Common Loon	Pink & White Lady's-Slipper	Red Pine
Oregon	February 14, 1859	Beaver State	Western Meadowlark	Oregon Grape	Douglas Fir
Kansas	January 29, 1861	Sunflower State	Western Meadowlark	Native Sunflower	Cottonwood
West Virginia	June 20, 1863	Mountain State	Cardinal	Big Rhododendron	Sugar Maple
Nevada	October 31, 1864	Silver State	Mountain Bluebird	Sagebrush	Single-Leaf Piñon
Nebraska	March 1, 1867	Cornhusker State	Western Meadowlark	Goldenrod	Cottonwood
Colorado	August 1, 1876	Centennial State	Lark Bunting	Rocky Mt. Columbine	Colorado Blue Spruce
North Dakota	November 2, 1889	Flickertail State	Western Meadowlark	Wild Prairie Rose	American Elm
South Dakota	November 2, 1889	Mount Rushmore State	Chinese Ring-Necked Pheasant	Pasqueflower	Black Hills Spruce
Montana	November 8, 1889	Treasure State	Western Meadowlark	Bitterroot	Ponderosa Pine
Washington	November 11, 1889	Evergreen State	Willow Goldfinch	Western Rhododendron	Western Hemlock
Idaho	July 3, 1890	Gem State	Mountain Bluebird	Syringa	White Pine
Wyoming	July 10, 1890	Equality State	Western Meadowlark	Indian Paintbrush	Plains Cottonwood
Utah	January 4, 1896	Beehive State	Seagull	Sego Lily	Blue Spruce
Oklahoma	November 16, 1907	Sooner State	Scissor-Tailed Flycatcher	Mistletoe	Redbud
New Mexico	January 6, 1912	Land of Enchantment	Roadrunner	Yucca	Piñon
Arizona	February 14, 1912	Grand Canyon State	Cactus Wren	Saguaro Cactus blossom	Paloverde
Alaska	January 3, 1959	Last Frontier	Willow Ptarmigan	Forget-me-not	Sitka Spruce
Hawaii	August 21, 1959	Aloha State	Nene (Hawaiian Goose)	Yellow Hibiscus	Kukui (Candlenut)

Time Line Questions

Use the time line to answer the following questions. Remember that "Uncle Sam" (The United States) was born in 1776.

1. How old was the United States when Texas became a state? _____

2. How many years after Vermont did California become a state? _____

3. Did any states join the Union (become part of the United States) ten years apart from each other? If yes, list the pairs of states and the ratification dates below.

    _____

    _____

4. Which of Wisconsin's neighbors (states sharing a border with Wisconsin) became a state before Wisconsin? _____

5. Which of Mississippi's neighbors became a state after Mississippi? _____

    _____

6. Which states joined the Union between 1810 and 1830? _____

    _____

    _____

7. How many states joined the Union in odd-numbered years? _____

8. How many states joined the Union in the 19th century? _____

9. The War of 1812 (against Britain) lasted from 1812 to 1814. What state(s) joined the Union during those years? _____

    The Mexican War lasted from 1846 to 1848. What state(s) joined the Union during those years? _____

    The American Civil War lasted from 1861 to 1865. What state(s) joined the Union during those years? _____

10. Sometimes several states joined the Union in a single year (for example: 1787, 1788, 1889). Other times, many years went by before another state was added. What is the longest period of time between the addition of new states? _____

UNITED STATES OF AMERICA

Answer Key

Alabama
Page 6: A = Andrew L = Lee A = Anniston B = Birmingham
A = Antebellum M = Montgomery A = azalea
Page 7: 1. false 2. A 3. four 4. D 5. Because it is in the middle of other Southern states. Answers will vary.

Alaska
Page 9: L = Arctic Ocean A = Pacific Ocean M = Beaufort Sea C = Bering Sea K = Gulf of Alaska B = Bristol Bay N = Cook Inlet F = Kotzebue Sound J = Norton Sound E = Prince William Sound G = Bering Strait I = Shelikof Strait D = Iliamna Lake H = Yukon River
Page 10: 1. false 2. D 3. 218 years 4. A 5. Answers will vary.

Arizona
Page 12:

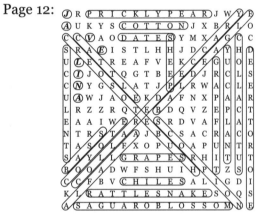

Solution: javelina

Page 13: 1. true 2. C 3. cotton, citrus fruit
4. B 5. You can tell what geological events happened in that location. Answers will vary.

Arkansas
Page 15: 1541 = M 1686 = O 1803 = C 1821 = K 1836 = I (Arkansas became a state)
1868 = N 1880 = G 1918 = B 1927 = I ("Great Flood") 1946 = R 1957 = D Solution: Mockingbird
Page 16: 1. false 2. A 3. in the middle 4. B 5. Flooding rivers carry silt to nearby areas. This adds minerals to the soil. Answers will vary.

California
Page 19:

Solution: California Condor

Page 20: 1. true 2. B 3. Sierra Nevada 4. B
5. There is gold for mining, a sunny, "golden" climate, and it is a destination for many people, including movie stars. Answers will vary.

Colorado
Page 22: C = Corners O = Ouray L = Lee O = oil R = Royal A = Aspen D = Denver O = Oro
Page 23: 1. false 2. A 3. Ute tribe 4. D 5. It was 100 years from the time the United States received its independence until the time Colorado became a state.

Answer Key

Connecticut

Page 25: A = Portable typewriter B = Repeating pistol C = Steamboat
D = Vulcanized rubber E = Semiconductor laser F = Sewing machine
G = Instant (Polaroid®) camera H = Weaving straw and silk together
I = Football tackling dummy
Page 26: 1. true 2. C 3. Hartford 4. A 5. 215,500 miles

Delaware

Page 28: 1. Leni-Lenape 2. 1609, English, The Netherlands 3. Wilmington 4. The
Netherlands 5. 1664 6. December 7, 1787 7. Sweden, The Netherlands, England, The United
States
Page 29: 1. false 2. B 3. Dover, Wilmington. 4. B 5. "Del" for Delaware, "Mar" for Maryland,
"Va" for Virginia. The peninsula is shared by all three states, so the name uses a part of each
state's name.

District of Columbia

Page 31: 1. Library of Congress, U.S. Capitol 2. Theodore Roosevelt Memorial 3. Arlington
National Cemetery, The Pentagon 4. The Washington Monument 5. The Washington
Monument, Thomas Jefferson Memorial 6. Vietnam War Veterans Memorial, Korean War
Veterans Memorial 7. The Lincoln Memorial
Page 32: 1. true 2. B 3. 24 years 4. C 5. Smithson was a scientist. Scientists usually strive to
acquire knowledge. At the Smithsonian, there are exhibits for art and design, science and
nature, and history and culture. By visiting the museum, people can learn about all of these
areas. Answers will vary.

Florida

Page 34: All answers are approximate. 1. 500,000 2. 16 million 3. No 4. 1900 and 1910; 1910
and 1920 5. 1980 and 1990 6. 4 million 7. 6 million 8. 1960-1990 9. 1930 10. 2000
Page 35: 1. true 2. C 3. Seminole tribe 4. C 5. A panhandle is a long, narrow strip of land
attached to a larger piece of land (like the handle of a pan). This description fits the top portion of Florida.

Georgia

Page 37:

Page 38: 1. true 2. A 3. peaches, peanuts,
pecans, tobacco (also cotton, sorghum,
soybeans, and wheat) 4. C 5. With an
easier way to process cotton, farmers
increased production. They probably
made more money. Answers will vary.

Hawaii

Page 40: H = Hawaii-Aleutian A = Archipelago W = Waialeale A = Arizona I = Iniki I = Iolani
Page 41: 1. true 2. B 3. British 4. C 5. Mountains in Hawaii are smoother, broader, and not as
tall, because the lava builds up around the base.

Idaho
Page 43:
Solution: Gem State

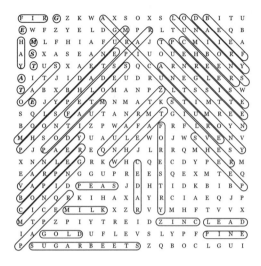

Page 44: 1. true 2. B 3. Nez Perce, Shoshone 4. B 5. Lewiston was probably named for Meriwether Lewis, who was part of the Lewis and Clark team that explored the area.

Illinois
Page 46: B = Bloomington G = Cairo D = Chicago A = De Kalb E = Dixon C = Springfield
F = Vandalia
Page 47: 1. true 2. D 3. Chicago, Springfield. Answers will vary. 4. D 5. Grains, meat, apples, machinery, and mining products (coal and oil) are transported by truck, train, or boat; travelers and tourists are transported by plane or car.

Indiana
Page 49: Car #1 (Robert) = 369 miles Car #2 (Kara) = 310 miles. The shortest trip is to go from Indianapolis to Terre Haute, back through Indianapolis to Fountain City, and back to Indianapolis again. Car #3 (the student) = 363 miles Car #4 (Alonzo) = 360 miles
Page 50: 1. false 2. A 3. Ohio River 4. A 5. It is at the center of the state.

Iowa
Page 52: 1. 1910-1930 2. After 1930-2000 3. 1930 4. hogs 5. hogs 6. cattle 7. 1990, $75
8. 1910, $5 9. 1990, $55 10. 1940, $5
Page 53: 1. true 2. B 3. flat, fertile 4. C 5. Corn syrup, cattle food, creamed corn, corn chips, tortillas, corn oil, etc. Answers will vary.

Kansas
Page 55: 1. Yates Center 2. Hiawatha 3. Topeka 4. Lawrence 5. Atchison 6. Colby
7. Oakley 8. Garden City 9. Fort Scott 10. Kinsley 11. Wichita 12. Wellington 13. Medicine Lodge 14. Johnson City 15. Independence 16. Topeka 17. Manhattan 18. Emporia
19. Cottonwood Falls Solution: The Wickedest Little City in America
Page 56: 1. false 2. D 3. Wichita 4. C 5. Kansas produces more wheat than any other state. So, Kansas fills America's "breadbasket."

Kentucky
Page 58: 1. Bowling Green 2. Black Mountain 3. Green River 4. Blue Licks Battlefield State Park 5. Black Patch War 6. Yellow-bellied Sapsucker 7. Pink Star 8. Yellow Poplar
9. Bluegill
Page 59: 1. false 2. B 3. tobacco 4. B 5. Bluegrass, which grows easily in Kentucky, has a slightly bluish tint.

Answer Key

Louisiana

Page 61: 1. J 2. E 3. A 4. N 5. L 6. A 7. F 8. F 9. I 10. T 11. E
Solution: Jean Laffite

Page 62: 1. true 2. B 3. Cajuns 4. A 5. The Mississippi River flows down the front of the "boot," like curly shoelaces.

Maine

Page 64:

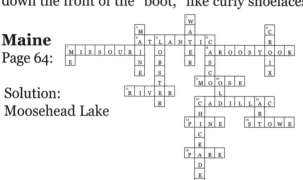

Solution:
Moosehead Lake

Page 65: 1. true 2. B 3. Quebec, New Brunswick 4. A 5. The trees were used for ship masts, because they were tall and straight.

Maryland

Page 67:

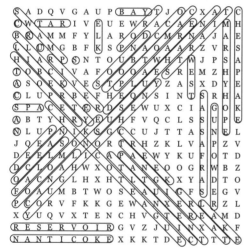

Page 68: 1. false 2. A 3. Eastern Shore, Western Shore 4. B 5. The capital would have been surrounded by states that were not part of the Union, which would have put it in danger of being taken over by the Confederate States. The Union was directed from Washington. If the capital had fallen, the Union may not have won the war.

Massachusetts

Page 70-71: Great Point Lighthouse lost its lifeboat on the night of the robbery. Nantucket Island was robbed.

Page 72: 1. true 2. C 3. Cape Cod 4. A 5. There are now many other ways to transport people and cargo.

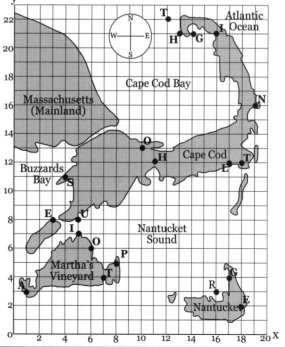

Answer Key

Michigan
Page 74: L U L L U L L U U U L L U U Solution: Kellogg and Post
Page 75: 1. false 2. D 3. iron ore 4. A 5. Early fur-traders traded wolverine pelts. Answers will vary.

Minnesota
Page 77: I = Lake Itasca A = Lake of the Woods L = Lake Superior H = Lake Winnibigoshish J = Leech Lake G = Lower Red Lake O = Minnesota River N = Mississippi River E = Rainy Lake D = Rainy River F = Red Lake River B = Red River M = St. Croix River K = St. Louis River C = Upper Red Lake
Page 78: 1. false 2. A 3. Mississippi River and Red River 4. A 5. "Minne" means water. Minneapolis is at the junction of two great rivers. Answers will vary.

Mississippi
Page 80: 1. 320 miles 2. 158 miles 3. Jackson to Ofahoma 4. Ofahoma and French Camp 5. 105 miles 6. 215 miles 7. Tupelo to Port Gibson; 113 miles
Page 81: 1. true 2. D 3. Jackson 4. D 5. If Vicksburg had been under Union control, Confederate troops would not have been able to use the Mississippi River to connect Confederate states in the north with Confederate states in the south. This would have weakened the Confederacy.

Missouri
Page 83:

Solution: The Missouri mule

Page 84: 1. false 2. D 3. Ozark Plateau or Ozarks or Ozark Mountains 4. C 5. It is at the junction of the Mississippi and Missouri Rivers. It was easier for fur traders to travel from the north to the south along these rivers.

Montana
Page 86: 1. Granite Peak, 12,600 feet; Mount Edith, 9,200 feet 2. Yes, Crazy Peak and Mount Cowan 3. 2 4. 5 5. 4, Crazy Peak, Froze-to-Death Mountain, Hollowtop Mountain, Mount Cowan 6. 2,900 feet 7. 700 feet 8. Mount Stimson and Froze-to-Death Mountain
page 87: 1. false 2. B 3. The United States and Great Britain 4. C 5. The "Treasure State" is appropriate for the gold, silver, and other metals found in the mountains. "Big Sky Country" is appropriate because of the view of the sky from the prairie portion of the state.

Nebraska
Page 89: N = Nebraska E = Equality B = Bellevue R = Railroad A = Arbor S = Sod K = Kearny A = Agate
Page 90: 1. true 2. B 3. continental 4. A 5. If the cattle overgraze, the grass does not grow back and the sand blows away.

Answer Key

Nevada
Page 92: H = Death Valley National Park U = Desert National Wildlife
Range M = Great Basin National Park B = Table Mountain
Wilderness Area O = Lake Mead National Recreation Area
L = Nellis Air Force Range D = Nevada Test Site T = Sheldon
National Wildlife Refuge Solution: Humboldt
Page 93: 1. true 2. B 3. The Colorado River 4. B 5. Fewer living things, including people, live in the area.

New Hampshire
Page 95: 1. chin 2. upper lip 3. upper lip 4. Answers will vary. 5. approximately 39' 6"
6. no, approximately 32-34' taller; about 6 giant human faces. Answers will vary.
Page 96: 1. false 2. D 3. Every four years, it holds the first presidential primary election.
4. D 5. It has several mountains named after U.S. presidents.

New Jersey
Page 98: 1. Hudson River 2. Staten Island, New York 3. Delaware River
4. Philadelphia, Pennsylvania 5. Delaware River
Page 99: 1. false 2. D 3. 46th largest 4. B 5. 1,020 more people live in each square mile of New Jersey than in the average U.S. square mile. It would take almost 14 square miles with the average U.S. population density to hold the same number of people as one New Jersey square mile.

New Mexico
Page 101: A. Big River = Rio Grande B. Wild River = Cimarron River C. Blood of Christ
Mountains = Sangre de Cristo Mountains D. Hens Mountains = Gallinas Mountains
1. The Cottonwood Trees = Los Alamos 2. Holy Faith = Santa Fe 3. The Meadows = Las Vegas
4. Help = Soccoro 5. The Fat Cottonwood Tree = Alamogordo 6. The Crosses = Las Cruces
Page 102: 1. false 2. C 3. 180,000 4. A 5. New Mexico was formerly a colony of Spain, then of
Mexico. It borders Mexico, a Spanish-speaking country.

New York
Page 103: A. 460,000 B. 2, 300,000 C. 920,000 D. 415,000 E. 350,000 F. 300,000
G. 3,520,000 H. 175,000 I. 150,000 J. 375,000 Most = Ireland Least = Denmark
Page 105: 1. true 2. A 3. Albany, New York City. Answers will vary. 4. C 5. An empire is a group
of states united under one state. Perhaps Washington thought that New York City, the New York
Harbor, and the Hudson River were very important for the growth and protection of the country.

North Carolina
Page 107: 1. Wilmington 2. Charlotte 3. Raleigh 4. Fayetteville 5. Jacksonville
6. Greensboro 7. Kannapolis 8. Asheville Solution: Ocracoke Island
Page 108: 1. true 2. D 3. west 4. D 5. From a distance, the mountaintops appear blue.

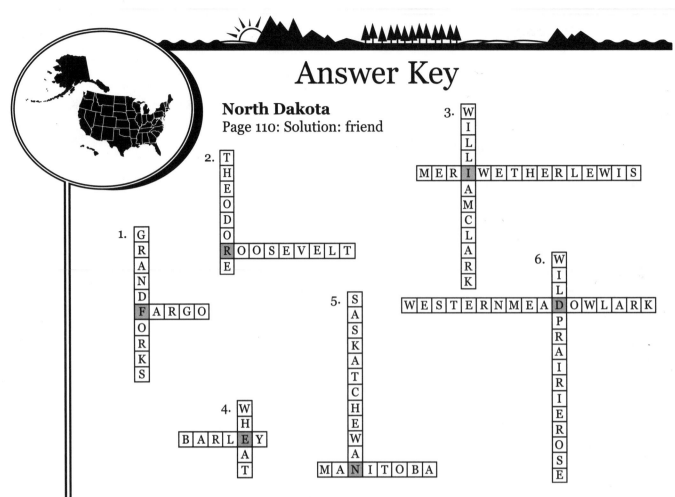

North Dakota

Page 110: Solution: friend

Page 111: 1. true 2. D 3. Fort Mandan 4. B 5. Cities formed and prospered along the river because the river made water available for drinking and irrigation. Since the river floods, the soil near it is more fertile for farming.

Ohio

Page 113: 1. M 2. P 3. E 4. H 5. C 6. G 7. I 8. N 9. F 10. L 11. Q 12. J 13. D 14. A 15. B 16. O 17. K

Page 114: 1. false 2. C 3. 16 4. D 5. 1,000 years = a millennium; 10 centuries = 1 millennium; 100 decades = 1 millennium

Oklahoma

Page 116: O = Oologah K = Kettle L = Leni-Lenape A = Act H = Harrison O = Okla M = Mistletoe A = Alphabet

Page 117: 1. true 2. D 3. panhandle 4. B 5. Inland because Tulsa is not near an ocean; seaport because Tulsa has access to the Gulf of Mexico from the Arkansas River.

Oregon

Page 119:
1. JOHNMCTOUGHTIN
2. JOHNMCTOUGHTHIN
3. JOHNMCFROMUGTHIN
4. THINJOHNMCFROMUG
5. THINJOHNECFROEUG
6. THINJOHNEFROEUG
7. THINJOHNEFOREUG
8. FATRONEFOREUG
9. FATREFOREUGON
10. FATERFOREUGON
11. FATERFOOREUGON
12. FATUERFOOREGON
13. FATUEROFOREGON
14. FATHER OF OREGON

Page 120: 1. false 2. D 3. the section to the west 4. C 5. They could plant trees to replace the ones cut down, and could avoid clear-cutting. Answers will vary.

Answer Key

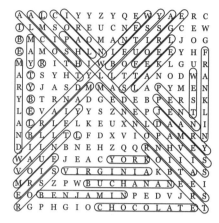

Pennsylvania

Page 122: Solution: Liberty Bell

Page 123: 1. true 2. A
3. Ohio or Delaware or
Susquehanna 4. A
5. It was the first state, so perhaps
it means that Pennsylvania was "key" to starting
the ratification process for all of the states.
Pennsylvania was located in the middle of the
original Thirteen Colonies, so it was in a "key"
location. Is it also where the Constitution and
the Declaration of Independence were written.

Rhode Island

Page 125: R = ratify H = Hope O = Oliver D = Dorr E = Eylandt I = Industrial
S = Sakonnet L = Light A = Antinomians N = Newport D = Dodge
Page 126: 1. true 2. C 3. Rhode Island 4. C 5. Yes; because they wanted more freedom,
Rhode Islanders resented interference from the British (including laws) that affected their
freedom.

South Carolina

Page 128: 1. Anderson 2. Greenville 3. Rock Hill 4. Camden 5. Florence 6. Myrtle Beach
7. Charleston 8. Hilton Head Island 9. Columbia. Best hole = Greenville (hole-in-one)
Worst holes = Hilton Head Island and Charleston (three over par)
Page 129: 1. true 2. A 3. Fort Sumter near Charleston, SC 4. D 5. Once the slaves were free,
farmers could not afford to pay enough laborers to work on their plantations.

South Dakota

Page 131: 1743 = D 1803 = Y 1861 = N 1868 = A 1874 = M 1889 = I 1927 = T 1947 = E
Solution = dynamite
Page 132: 1. false 2. D 3. corn, wheat, soybeans 4. B 5. Washington was the first president, and
helped win independence from the British as an army general. Jefferson wrote *The Declaration
of Independence.* Lincoln helped to end slavery. Theodore Roosevelt started the national land
conservation effort.

Tennessee

Page 134: All answers are approximate. 1. Kentucky; 336 miles 2. Missouri; 56 miles 3. Virginia,
Alabama, Georgia, Mississippi, Missouri 4. Mississippi, Alabama, Georgia; 336 5. Kentucky,
Virginia; 448 miles 6. northern; 112 7. About 1,236 miles 8. Because it probably wraps around
the mountains. Answers will vary.
Page 135: 1. false 2. B 3. cotton, tobacco 4. D 5. Answers will vary.

 CD-0774 50 States

Answer Key

Texas

Page 137: 1. Dwight Eisenhower 2. Mildred "Babe" Didrikson Zaharias 3. Lyndon Johnson 4. Buddy Holly 5. John Garner 6. Audie Murphy 7. Juan Cortina

Page 138: 1. true 2. D 3. oil 4. D 5. Stephen Austin started early American settlements in Texas. Sam Houston led the army which won independence from Mexico.

Utah

Page 140: 1. 28% 2. 29%; 18% 3. Heavy or frequent rain; more water would decrease the salinity. 4. 19%; 12% 5. The North Arm is more salty. It receives less freshwater to dilute the salt. 6. 1984 and 1997; 17%

Page 141: 1. true 2. A 3. Wasatch Mountains, Uinta Mountains 4. A 5. Drawings will vary.

Vermont

Page 143: The New York traveler went to the Brattleboro sugarhouse and bought maple syrup. The New Hampshire traveler went to the St. Johnsbury sugarhouse and bought maple fudge. The Quebec traveler went to the St. Albans sugarhouse and bought sugar-on-snow.

Page 144: 1. true 2. D 3. granite, marble, slate 4. B 5. Rural population: two-thirds of 600,000 = 400,000. Urban population : one-third of 600,000 = 200,000. 40,000 of these people live in Burlington. 200,000 - 40,000 = 160,000 people who live in cities or towns other than Burlington.

Virginia

Page 146:

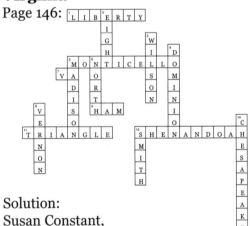

Solution:
Susan Constant,
Godspeed, and
Discovery

Page 147: 1. false 2. A 3. Richmond 4. C 5. Diversified means varietized. In this case, it means that Virginia relies on many different industries. It is good because if one industry fails (for example, crops die because of bad weather), the economy still has other industries which can help keep people employed.

Washington

Page 149: sea otter, Roosevelt elk, Licorice Fern, Ponderosa Pine, Douglas Fir, grizzly bear, steelhead trout, sockeye salmon, jumping mouse, spotted owl, mountain caribou, banana slug, Sitka Spruce, killer whale Solution: Evergreen State

Page 150: 1. false 2. B 3. salmon 4. B 5. The Puget Sound is protected so that ships can land safely. Washington is on the Pacific Ocean, which makes trading with Asia cheaper and more practical.

Answer Key

West Virginia

Page 152: W = Wheeling E = Elk S = soft T = Thomas V = Vandalia
I = Isaac R = Romney G = Grave I = Island N = New I = iron A = Abe
Page 153: 1. false 2. B 3. Mountain State 4. A 5. If the Union gained control of the B&O Railroad, Confederate troops and supplies would no longer be able to travel by train.

Wisconsin

Page 155: 1. mozzarella 2. other American 3. 2.2% 4. 92.1% 5. 3.2% 6. Other Italian would be 7.6% of the pie chart, and Asiago would be 3.5% of the pie chart.
Page 156: 1. false 2. D 3. Lake Michigan, Lake Superior 4. A 5. Water routes were more direct. Traders could carry many more furs by boat than by horseback. Also, there were few roads, and many trees created obstacles.

Wyoming

Page 158: 1. D 2. I 3. L 4. N 5. M 6. A 7. O 8. T 9. U 10. T Solution: Old Man of the Mountain
Page 159: 1. false 2. B 3. 1890 4. A 5. The deeper the water, the more pressure there is. Geysers that have deeper sources will have higher eruptions.

The United States of America

Page 160:

Solution: Alaska and Hawaii

Planting Pie Charts

Page 161: 1. Iowa, Minnesota 2. Kansas, Missouri 3. Corn would be most affected; almost half the corn wouldn't be grown. Sorghum would be least affected; only 18% of the sorghum wouldn't be grown. 4. Yes, 1% 5. No 6. No. Nebraska produced 10% of the total corn and 7% of the total sorghum. From the pie charts alone, it is not possible to tell what the totals are. The text at the top of the page shows that 40 times more corn is produced than sorghum, but this information isn't available from the pie charts.

Answer Key

American Borders

Page 162: 1. Canada: ME, NH, VT, NY, MI, MN, ND, MT, ID, WA, AK, Mexico: TX, NM, AZ, CA Russia: no states 2. Arctic: AK
Pacific: AK, HI, WA, OR, CA Atlantic: TX, LA, MS, AL, FL, GA, SC, NC, VA, DE, MD, NJ, NY, CT, MA, RI, NH, ME; Border Gulf: 5
3. Great Lakes: NY, PA, OH, IN, IL, MI, WI, MN 4. Mississippi River: MN, WI, IA, IL, MO, KY, TN, AR, MS, LA 5. Missouri: IA, IL, KY, TN, AR, OK, KS, NE Massachusetts: VT, NH, NY, CT, RI Mississippi: TN, AL, LA, AR Oregon: WA, ID, NV, CA South Dakota: ND, MN, IA, NE, WY, MT 6. Nation's Capital: MD, VA

Temperature Trends

Page 163: 1. 51°F 2. 13°F 3. 31°F 4. 39°F 5. Nebraska, Nebraska 6. Florida, Texas, southern 7. Minnesota, Washington, northern 8. Florida, 22°, southern 9. Minnesota, 62°, northern 10. Southern states are warmer, and there is less variation in temperature between seasons. Northern states are cooler, and there is more variation in temperature between seasons.

Time Line Questions

Page 165: 1. 69 years 2. 59 years 3. Arkansas (1836) and Iowa (1846); Wisconsin (1848) and Minnesota (1858) 4. Illinois (1818), Michigan (1837), and Iowa (1846) 5. Alabama (1819) and Arkansas (1836) 6. Louisiana, Indiana, Mississippi, Illinois, Alabama, Maine, Missouri
7. 23 8. 29 9. War of 1812 = Louisiana (1812); Mexican War = Iowa (1846), Wisconsin (1848); American Civil War = Kansas (1861), West Virginia (1863), Nevada (1864)
10. 47 years (between Arizona in 1912, and Alaska in 1959)